▰ *SOUTHERNER*

Southerner

BY CHARLES LONGSTREET WELTNER

🏴 *United States Congressman from Atlanta*

J. B. LIPPINCOTT COMPANY

Philadelphia and New York

TO MY FATHER

SOUTHERNER

PART ONE

1

The Speaker of the House of Representatives, John W. McCormack of Massachusetts, slammed down his gavel. "Evidently a sufficient number. The Ayes and Nays are ordered." It was July 2, 1964, and the occasion was the final passage of the Civil Rights Bill. "Those who are in favor of adopting the Senate amendments and passing the bill will, when their names are called, vote 'Aye.' Those opposed will vote 'No.'" The galleries were packed to capacity. Outside in the halls were scores of people who had been unable to find seats. "The Clerk will call the roll."

"Abbitt." "No."

"Abernethy." "No."

"Addabbo." "Aye." ...

In February of that year, the House, after months of controversy and days of nerve-racking, exhausting debate, had passed the bill, styled H.R. 7152, by a vote of 290 to 130. Then it had gone to the Senate, where it had been debated for 93 days, longer than any other bill in the Senate's history. Finally, a two-thirds majority of Senators had demanded cloture, and the bill, somewhat changed, had been passed by 81 votes to 19. Now it had come back to the House for the last step—final passage.

... "Huddleston." "No."

"Hull." "No."
"Hutchinson." "Aye." ...
In a few minutes, the Clerk would near the end of the roll. He would call my name, and I would have to answer. Whatever I said then would be recorded forever. There would be no "Yes, maybe" or "No, but." The vote would be just "Aye" or "No," and there the matter would stand for all who wished to see, for all time to come.
... "Mahon." "No."
"Mailliard." "Aye."
"Marsh." "No." ...
The debates, the angry exchanges, the charges and countercharges, the mountains of mail, the editorials, the speeches, the marches, the demonstrations—all that was over now. The issue, between the fervent hope for a new order and equally fervent devotion to the old, was now to be decided—in this chamber.
... "Patman." "No."
"Patten." "Aye."
"Pelly." "Aye." ...
The nation had agonized over this decision since June of the preceding year. A part of that agony had been mine. As a Southerner, it was hard for me to contemplate the changes that were being sought. But as an American, I knew that manifest wrongs to a substantial number of the nation's people required a remedy.
... "Tuck." "No."
"Tupper." "Aye."
"Tuten." "No." ...
In a moment I would be recorded on one side of the issue or the other. The choice was mine, and though I would gladly have avoided it, it had to be made. Now.

... "Watts." "No."
"Weaver." "Aye."
"*Weltner.*" "*Aye.*"

There have been many changes in the South since that day, and many more are to come. This, then, is a small comment on those changes by one who loves the South, and who has had a part, however small, in bringing them about.

* * *

The place to begin is at the beginning. The beginning for me was in Atlanta "early on a frosty morn" in 1927. My father, a lawyer, was the son of a Lutheran minister. My mother was one of a large family that had long been active in Georgia affairs. And I was the youngest of five children. We grew up in a big house on the Northside with plenty of growing room. Far back at the end of the lot was a rotting old structure that had once been part of the county prison farm. It was our "haunted house," and we frequently scared ourselves with stories of ghosts returning to the scene of their miseries and indignities, to wreak revenge upon their former captors, or anyone else in sight.

There was room for dogs, chickens, horseshoes, grape arbors, bamboo patches, lean-tos, dugouts, pole vault pits, swings, tree houses, and anything else that young imaginations could conjure up. It was a fine place to grow.

In 1932 my father became the first Chancellor of the Board of Regents of the University System of Georgia, a post that had come into being largely as a result of his own efforts in reorganizing and consolidating the numerous colleges and normal schools that served as higher educational facilities for young Georgians. His new duties required much travel, and frequently he took me with him. We would go in his old Ford automobile, plying the Georgia roads from one school to the next. That was in the depth of the Depression, when life in the city was hard, and life on the farm well-nigh impossible. I remember the raw hills of the countryside, the dilapidated shanties strung along the road, the dank filling stations and the smell of gasoline, the men in overalls, the women in feed-sack dresses.

The people we called on talked endlessly about "the University," "the System," "Board of Regents," and other things that were no more to me than sounds. Restless and impatient, I would fret to be under way. But the talk would continue. When finally we would move toward our car, they would follow and, foot on running board, continue about "the Regents" and "the System."

I remember some names and some faces. I remember some places and some incidents. But I remember only one conversation, of all those to which I was captive. One night a tall, gaunt man followed us out of a school building. "Chancellor," he said, "we can't vote for you for governor. But if you ever run for President, you can sho' count on us." He was the head of a Negro college.

It was during that time I first entered politics. After supper in the summertime my mother would move us out of the house to run off energy before bedtime. We would catch lightning bugs, and play sling the statue, red light, and another game called "ain't no boogerbears out tonight." One summer we spent evenings shouting from the sidewalk to every car that passed, "Vote for Roosevelt!" Of course, I didn't know who Roosevelt was, or why anyone should vote for him, or what voting was. But it was politics. And of recent years I have noted little boys, about the same age as I was then, shouting to me on early summer evenings as I drive by. Sometimes they tell me to vote for my opponent.

When I was eleven years old, and in high school, the War came. My brother went into the Army, where he was to spend five years, and my sisters, whose husbands had gone away to war, came home again. My interests in those days covered many things—Scouting, tennis, history (my father gave me $25 to read Nehru's book, *Glimpses of World History*), the old Confederacy, and girls.

The Confederacy had a particular appeal to me, and I moved into that peculiar "Confederate period" experienced by many Southern lads, and endured by many non-Southerners. With a Confederate general for a great-grandfather, and an ample supply of family relics at hand, I suppose my case was more virulent than most. The Great War was the golden age of all history. My heroes were the heroes of that day—Robert E. Lee, J. E. B. Stewart, Stonewall Jackson, John Singleton Mosby, and others of the Confederate pantheon.

And, indeed, there is still for most of us in the South a certain inexplicable appeal from those days. They combined all the elements of gallantry, chivalry, courage, and Greek tragedy that have fascinated modern man for centuries. The early days of that war, bringing victory after victory to an outnumbered and machineless South, made the defeat that followed even more crushing. The courage of Southern men and women, in the face of impossible odds, cast about the whole era a glow that even the underlying shame of slavery cannot dim. It was easy to become somewhat pixilated about the Old South, lauding its virtues, and overlooking its shortcomings. I was no exception—and, to some extent, remain under its spell.

When I was fifteen, the trustees of Oglethorpe University asked my father to take charge of their school. Oglethorpe is a small college now located just north of Atlanta. Its first incarnation began in Milledgeville, Georgia, in 1831, and lasted some thirty years, until its student body became Confederate infantry and its endowment Confederate bonds. Sidney Lanier, poet, musician, and soldier, is its most famous alumnus. In the 1940's, another war had called its students, and the school was saddled with a mountain of debt. Most of its faculty had departed. Its academic rating was nil. For nine years my father served as its president, collecting a first-rate faculty, retiring the debt, and gaining academic accreditation. It was a monumental achievement, and a work of dedication. For all those years, he served without a salary.

I entered Oglethorpe at sixteen. My education came partly in the classrooms, partly from the first-rate professors who now served the school, and partly from a wide and somewhat irrational curiosity on many subjects. Three years later, I was admitted to Columbia University Law School.

I went north with my Southern background, and returned three years later with it all intact and totally unimpaired. At the age of nineteen, I boarded the *Southerner*, bound for New York. The train arrived at Pennsylvania Station at one o'clock on a Sunday afternoon. My dormitory, Army Hall, was on 125th Street, in what had once been an orphanage. It was the repository of an overflow student body from surrounding schools, and its inmates called it "Army Hell." The first light of day visible to me in New York City was the breathtaking panorama of the Broadway and 125th Street subway stop.

I found the study of law fairly interesting, but what really fascinated me was a type of student I had never encountered before—one all aquiver with social intensities. I viewed the law as pretty much law, and foresaw the practice of law to be the pragmatic process of winning cases for clients. There was a substantial minority among my classmates who deemed it no such, but an instrument of their concepts of social justice and a means to right their choice of social wrongs. They would agonize over the logic and reasoning of legal opinions, and would castigate in severest terms those judges with whom they disagreed.

The three Southerners in my class became fast friends, easily maintaining our natural superiority over those lesser breeds born north of the Line.

It was at Columbia that I learned to politick. The secret is fairly simple—you try to be friendly and polite to everyone. A Southern accent won me the vice-presidency of my freshman class, although it failed me in a bid for the presidency of my legal fraternity. The successful candidate managed to nominate all three Southerners for the post, thus splitting the Southern bloc and dividing our friends.

After my second year at Columbia, I took the Georgia bar examination—and waited. Late that August I came home to the good news. At twenty-one years of age, I was now a member of the bar, and my own man—as soon as my father finished paying for the one year remaining at Columbia.

Graduation was in June, and I came home, ready for

17

the accolades of an eager and affluent clientele, and an openhanded reception by an appreciative bar.

That September, Betty Jean Center and I were married, and began housekeeping in a third-floor, walkup efficiency apartment in Atlanta.

I shall always recall my first day of practice. I was offered a place with a firm in Atlanta at $100 per month, plus one-half of all the fees I brought in, which was $100 per month better than the next best offer I had received. I reported to work, ready to win fame and fortune. One of the partners, however, had had other ideas about hiring me, and he was headman in the office that day. Dutifully I inquired as to his pleasure. "Why, yes," he said, "there is something you can do. Let me show you." We went back to a corridor crammed with several years' worth of loose-leaf tax supplements. "See those?" he asked, pointing. "You can dust those up for us." I dusted, and left to accept the next best offer.

Law is a wonderful profession. It calls out the very best within any serious practitioner. The skillful and conscientious advocate must be a master of many trades. He must combine science, philosophy, medicine, psychiatry, and any number of other arts upon occasion. His mind must be attuned to each situation he encounters, and capable of grasping any discipline in a minimum of time. He must be eloquent, persuasive, humble, self-assured, determined, and reasonable, and he must know how to charge—and collect—a fee.

Like all other young lawyers, I was waiting for the "Big Case." Then one day I thought it had come. Pinkie Smith, a trusted and valued Negro employee of the state of Georgia, had great confidence in the senior partner of my firm, former Governor Ellis Arnall. One day in 1953, he called to report a tragedy. His little grandson had been struck by a car and had died at the hospital. I took the case, and worked hard on it.

After months of preliminaries, we went to trial. The case took several hours to try, and finally the jury retired. Then came the worst part—waiting for the verdict. I have been through that agony many times, and there is no way to describe it. A good lawyer puts his heart and soul, along with a great investment of time, into a case. When all the argument is over, and all the testimony concluded, and all the charges delivered, he can only wait.

And so we waited, making small talk, walking the corridor, speaking to passers-by. About two hours later a newsboy came by with the afternoon edition of the *Atlanta Journal*. The headline read: "SUPREME COURT OUTLAWS SEGREGATION IN PUBLIC SCHOOLS." The date was, of course, May 17, 1954.

My own "Big Case" ended with a hung jury. But on the same day, another court had spoken loud and clear. For me, and for many other Southerners, that day was the beginning of a long and sometimes weary self-appraisal. Thinking Southerners were required to re-examine—or, in many cases, to make an initial examination—of their views on the race question.

My early days were somewhat removed from an awareness of strife or difficulties. Labor disputes, political foment, and racial tensions were somewhere else. Now, there was this decision. What did this mean to the South? What did it mean to Southern education, to Southern social patterns, to Southern politics? The issue was raised, and had to be answered in every Southern mind.

Like all other Southern lads, I had "known" Negroes. As a small child, I had played with a few. I knew boys from Irbytown, Johnsontown, Bagley Park, and other enclaves in the community. I grew up with a succession of Negro maids, each one of whom was practically part of the family. I knew Joe—at the filling station a half mile away. (At that time, I was afflicted with bicycle tires that had a slow leak, requiring daily attention. Joe used to call me his "best air customer." It was a good excuse for examining the large selection of penny candy—jawbreakers, striped coconut bars, and those peanut-shaped things that tasted like banana oil.)

I had been in Negro homes. Sometimes when Eva, or Annie, or another of our maids was sick, my mother took me with her to visit and provide groceries. Down rutted roads, strewn with automobile tires, bedsprings, and rotting mattresses, we would go, to enter a miserable hovel that passed for home. At Christmas and Thanksgiving, we would deliver baskets and toys to a needy family. The little ones would come out of the house, or from under the porch, and hang onto their mother's cotton dress, eyes big and black, wondering about these white folks who came.

I knew Molly and Murray, the maid and janitor of the grammar school I had attended for seven years. I knew Clifford, at Oglethorpe, a first-rate dog man who took care of my huge redbone hound, "Cinnamon."

But there was no race problem—at least insofar as I was concerned. Negroes were poor. They lived somewhere else. We helped them when we could through churches and personal charity. And that was about it.

There was no race problem—until the Supreme Court

came along in 1954, and, by a few words, changed the pattern of centuries.

Old sores were in an instant rubbed raw, and old wounds were ripped open. Public reaction to the decision was cataclysmic. Not a single responsible public voice was heard in its support. Every officeholder felt compelled to point out its manifold evils. The speeches rolled. The state legislature was in a frenzy of reaction. Citizens organized. Resolutions were passed. Memorials were framed. In Congress, of course, the Southern Manifesto went the rounds. Lawyers argued the content of the decision, its legitimacy, impact, and style. The Attorney General of Georgia promptly denounced it as "illegal." The impeachers tried to impeach. Interposition was exhumed from the Sedition Act days. The Ku Klux Klan stirred from its slumber. The White Citizens Council sprang into bloom. In Georgia, the legislature created something called the Georgia Education Commission, designed to preach segregation at taxpayers' expense. Rallies were held. The populace was aroused.

And through it all, I remember only one of my friends who was willing to say that the Supreme Court was right. Jack Turner was my contemporary at the bar. One morning at the drugstore once located at Five Points, we were drinking coffee with a young assistant to the state Attorney General. The latter was most vehement in his agreement with his employer. "The Court is wrong. It is an illegal decision! They have no power to amend the Constitution," and so forth. I asked, "Who's to say that the Court is wrong other than the Court? Where is the appeal?" Jack took another, far more forthright and honest position. "I think they're right," he said. I rested on purely procedural grounds. He accepted it as a mandate of conscience.

But it would be a long time before the 1954 decision had any practical application in Georgia.

❊   ❊   ❊

Nineteen fifty-four was an important year for me. It was then that I first took an active part in elective politics. In June of that year, a young man I greatly admired announced for Congress, opposing the incumbent, James C. Davis, who had held the Fifth District Congressional seat since 1946.

Morris B. Abram was a native of Ben Hill County, Georgia. He was an honor graduate of the University of Georgia, and a Rhodes scholar. He was clearly the most brilliant young mind in the legal profession in Georgia, and he had already earned an enviable reputation for sagacity and eloquence.

When Abram announced, I put myself at his service. The Fifth District then consisted of three counties—Fulton, DeKalb, and Rockdale. At the incumbent's direction, the County Unit System was applied to the primary election. Under this arrangement, the two big counties, Fulton and DeKalb, had six unit votes each, and Rockdale County, population 8,464 (1950 census), had two unit votes. Whoever received a plurality (not necessarily a majority) of the votes within each county received the entire unit vote accorded to that county.

James Davis had come to Congress in 1946 by carrying pluralities in his home county of DeKalb and in Rockdale. He had lost Fulton County and lost the over-all popular vote by 10,000 votes to the previous incumbent. Yet he had won eight unit votes to her six, and he went to Congress. In 1952 the same thing had happened. He had won again on unit votes, again losing the over-all popular vote.

In the days of turmoil over the Supreme Court's decision, the County Unit System was hailed as the last and best protection against the "bloc vote." A few years earlier, the white primary had met its demise at the hands of the Federal Court. Negroes could now vote in the Democratic primary, which was about all the voting we had in Georgia then. So the chief virtue of the County Unit System was, according to its adherents, its ability "to stop the nigger vote at the county line." Because the greatest concentration of Negro voters was found in Atlanta, the Unit System did just that. It also stopped *my* vote at the county line.

Abram made the Unit System his chief campaign issue in 1954. He spent months on the circuit. He organized precincts, spoke at innumerable coffees, shook hands, and appeared on television. I helped him as I could. My wife and I sponsored a neighborhood meeting for him. She made telephone calls. I substituted for him on the speaking circuit and contributed a few dollars to his campaign. He lost.

There was then, and is now, a strange white reaction to Negro voting patterns. The most ardent and vociferous racist can spend weeks inflaming racial passions, preach a white-heat brand of white supremacy, embrace the Ku Klux Klan, and spur it on to greater achievement, and repeat time and again that he wants no Negroes voting for *him!* Then he will solemnly warn the constituency that his opponent will receive the "bought, black, bloc vote." The

23

voters are supposed to believe that Negro unanimity, in such a case, is certain proof of scandalous misdeeds and political skulduggery.

Those were difficult days. Agitation over the Supreme Court and the "bloc vote," suspicions heightened by the McCarthy heyday—all served to arouse public passion. There was little, if any, counsel of reason and restraint in public. The Georgia legislature, following the lead of other Southern states, adopted the massive-resistance approach, packing the statute books with school-closing laws. It was even deemed necessary to provide for felony convictions for any public official who might approve funds for a non-segregated educational facility. Thus the trap was set. The state of Georgia and the government of the United States were on a collision course. The only question was when the two would meet.

Georgia politics remained Georgia politics, except more so. The issue in the gubernatorial race for 1954 was "segregation and the County Unit System." The question was who was most for them—for never a syllable was uttered against either. Marvin Griffin was elected by an overwhelming county unit vote, although two-thirds of the people of Georgia voted against him.

The situation changed little over the next four years. Griffin was successful in maintaining both the County Unit System and segregation. I had completed my two years in the Army, and returned to the law practice. My wife had patiently borne the early penury of the private law practitioner, and we had three small children.

In the 1958 governor's race the issue was again "segregation and the County Unit System."

By then, Little Rock had happened. Governor Faubus

had called out the Guard. President Eisenhower had called out the paratroopers. The school had closed its doors. And education had suffered a staggering blow. Now, with one child in public school and another soon to enter kindergarten, we began to wonder what would happen in Georgia. It was clear what the state politicians intended. New school-closing laws were added periodically, along with resolutions for the impeachment of the Supreme Court and memorials to Congress. No matter what scheme was proposed, it was assured of passage "if it will help preserve our Southern way of life."

The leading candidate for governor of Georgia in 1958 was Lieutenant Governor Ernest Vandiver, who struck the keynote of his campaign in what soon came to be known as his "No, not one" speech. In this speech he vowed with all the firmness at his command to preserve both segregation and the County Unit System, to resist the "tyranny" of the Supreme Court at every crossroad and every hamlet in Georgia, and to preserve segregated public education by going to jail, if necessary. He assured the voters that "No, not one" Negro child would ever enter a white school! Nonetheless, he was attacked by his opponent, a Baptist minister from Ty Ty, Georgia, as being weak on segregation.

It was in this state of public affairs that I became associated with Morris Abram in a great adventure—the abolition of the County Unit System.

I have noted how that system affected Congressional races in the Fifth District of Georgia. Its impact upon the whole state was even more traumatic. Since 1917, the law of Georgia had required that all primaries for the offices of U. S. Senator, governor, lieutenant governor, and other state house posts be conducted under a County Unit System. In this scheme the eight largest counties in the state were accorded six unit votes each, the next 30 in population were given four, and the remaining 121 counties, two each. Whoever amassed a plurality of county unit votes, by carrying pluralities within counties, was the nominee. And the nominee of the Democratic primary was, in practice, the winner of the election.

Fulton County, with over half a million people, had but three times the county unit votes of Echols County, with 1,875 people. Thus, one vote in Echols County was worth about one hundred votes in Fulton County.

The inequities to be related from this system are endless. It is quite obvious that Atlantans had no voice whatsoever in their state government, or in the choice of U. S. Senators, and practically none in the choice of a Congressman. The legislature of Georgia was structured on about the same basis, so there was no relief to be had there. I well recall the comment of one south Georgia legislator on a proposal just to *study* the system. "Why," he declared in horror, "I could never vote for that. It would dilute the vote of the folks in Brooks County, Georgia!" At that time, a vote in Brooks County was worth eleven votes in Fulton County.

Morris Abram had an old dream—to destroy the County Unit System completely and forever. I shared that dream, and had done some slight work in opposing proposed state constitutional amendments that would have extended the system to the general election—amendments which were defeated overwhelmingly by the popular vote of the people of Georgia.

When James Davis had first been "elected" by the Unit

System, Abram had tested the system in the Supreme Court of the United States. The Court had held that the election was over, and the issue was "moot." Two years later, Abram had mounted two more efforts. The Supreme Court of Georgia had found nothing wrong with the system, and the Supreme Court of the United States had declared that there was no "Federal question" involved.

Now, in 1958, it was time to try again. There were three new members on the high court. Two Justices had dissented from the majority before, expressing themselves against the system. If the three new Justices joined the two dissenters, there would be a majority in favor of outlawing the system.

Our problem was to find a new theory upon which to base a new suit.

My first dealing with the United States Congress was to order two copies of the recently passed Civil Rights Act of 1957. It was my hope that it might contain something—anything—upon which we could hang our hat—and, indeed, it did. Three words had been added to the U. S. Code, Title 28. That law forbade any person, under color of office, to deprive any other person of his civil rights. The 1957 Act added the words, "including voting rights." We seized upon this as the new hook, and argued that Congress had specifically extended the old statute to include voting rights.

Abram found a plaintiff to challenge the state crowd in the upcoming Democratic primary—none other than the old war-horse foe of the Unit System, and of everything else that incurred his displeasure, Mayor William B. Hartsfield.

It was my job to draft the petition, assemble the exhibits, and interpret our statistical data. This I did, sitting up late every night. It was painful work, because a severe shoulder wrench had almost incapacitated my writing arm. But I loved it. I drew new and horrendous conclusions from new population data, penning the phrases that would spell, I hoped, doom for County Unitry in Georgia. I even changed the title of one chart from "Discrimination Ratio" to "Disparity Factor," to avoid any misinterpretations. And finally it was done.

We would proceed through a three-judge court. Only such a panel can enjoin the act of a state official, and only through such an injunction could we hope to win.

It was on a cold Saturday morning in March that Abram, two of his associates, and I sought to file the petition. Judge Boyd Sloan was in his office in Gainesville, Georgia, 50 miles north of Atlanta. We arrived there at eleven in the morning, to a polite but cool reception. The judge knew our purpose, and obviously did not welcome the prospects. He ordered the petition filed, withholding judgment on whether he would call for the three-judge panel. And there things rested. Time went by. The judge did not rule. Finally, Judge Sloan ordered a hearing on whether or not the case should proceed. In due time he ruled—against us, holding as in the earlier case that there was no substantial Federal question. Yet, I must acknowledge that, slow as it seemed, Judge Sloan protected our rights in the matter, ruling in time to make subsequent action possible.

Now we appealed to the Supreme Court. The brief was written and printed, and flown to Washington for filing. A motion to expedite was submitted, and again we waited. May came, and went. The Court had only three weeks more to sit before adjournment. Finally, they ruled against us by a vote of five to four. But we had kept Justices Douglas and Black, and added Justices Warren and Brennan. All we needed was one more vote, and some day the Court was bound to change.

And we had had one great consolation in coming so close. A few days before the decision was handed down, a rumor had spread around the state capitol that we had won. State house officers, elected or appointed by or under the Unit System, were thrown into a panic, sensing the awesome might of all those voters in the urban counties lying in wait at the next election, ready to recall the sins committed against the population centers of our state in the quest of two-unit votes. Their agitation was most gratifying.

The 1958 gubernatorial race meanwhile proceeded, and Ernest Vandiver was elected by an awesome majority. The "No, not one" speech, together with the gross inadequacies of his opponent, had done the job. Georgia settled down to enact a few refinements to the school-closing laws, and turned its attention to farm-to-market roads, hog cholera, and other matters of moment. Bloc voters of the evil city machines were safely hedged about by the beneficent restraints of the County Unit System, and all was right with the world.

The law practice was providing me with a good living, and politics once again became somewhat remote.

But what the Supreme Court had said on May 17, 1954, had not been forgotten. Slowly cases came to the fore in other Southern states. And after all the smoke had cleared, the law prevailed. It was bound to come to Georgia, and the lessons from Little Rock, New Orleans, and Virginia were quite clear. Then a suit was filed, seeking the admission of Negro children to previously all-white schools in Atlanta, and the issue came to a head. What we were told "couldn't happen here" was about to happen.

The idea of desegregated schools was difficult to approach. There were always many voices ready to demand, at the slightest provocation, "Do you want your daughter to marry a nigger?" There was no open discussion of the vital issue that Georgians had to face sooner or later. If something did not happen to prevent it, the entire educational system of the Atlanta area would be scuttled, without so much as one voice raised in protest.

Finally, one hardy soul spoke. M. M. ("Muggsy") Smith was a long-time member of the Georgia legislature. He sold insurance for a living, and his wife was with the Atlanta school system. He addressed the Parent-Teacher Association at Spring Street School, and the title of his remarks was "Spring Street School for Sale." Muggsy did nothing more than to point out that under the law, neither Spring Street School nor any other school could be operated once it was required by Federal court order to admit a Negro pupil. If such an order were issued, state statutes made provision for the sale of the school property to private bidders. Muggsy simply wanted everyone to know that Spring Street School was for sale, or shortly would be.

There was immediate protest. A cross was burned on Smith's lawn. Someone tried to bomb his house. He was condemned as a scalawag, Communist, mongrelizer, bolshevik, and all the other epithets that signify disagreement. But Muggsy Smith was right. His courage, in simply saying what everybody should have known but what no one wished to know, laid bare the issue.

Shortly thereafter, a group of Atlantans, many of whom had waged and lost battles for worthy causes in the past, bestirred themselves. They came up with an organization called "Help Our Public Education (HOPE)." HOPE said, by name, activity, and membership, "You are just about to destroy a multimillion-dollar education system, and we won't stand for it." I joined at an early date, being fascinated with the prospect of waging law against the school-closers and the County-Unit and wool-hat types, and winning. My task, as one of the lawyers involved, was to prepare suits attacking school closings from every possible avenue.

We were, of course, castigated as a bunch of integrators trying to mislead the people. The school-closers had a strange outlook: "We can win this fight for our schools, our children, and our way of life," they maintained, "if we just try!" HOPE soon generated an opposing organization called the "Metropolitan Association for Continued Segregated Education," or, for short, MACSE (pronounced "mace"). When HOPE distributed stickers for car windows reading, "We Want Public Education," the closers countered with a sticker of their own that said, "Me, Too— But Segregated." Apparently it never occurred to them, even in the face of Little Rock and New Orleans and a pending suit in the Northern District of Georgia, that it was impossible to *have* both.

But the two groups battled it out on the periphery of the public mind. Most people still refused to be bothered by the situation, or to take the time to consider the alternatives. HOPE's main approach was to try to "mold public opinion." I considered this a futile effort, for several reasons. The first was, of course, the County Unit System. Because Atlanta was the locus of the pending school litigation, other areas were not immediately concerned. Because Atlanta was politically impotent, its problems never received due attention from either the legislature or the governor. The governor had spoken his mind on the subject ("No, not one"), and the state legislature was hard after him. Fulton County, with 15 per cent of the population, had less than 2 per cent of the votes in the legislature. The state politicians were eagerly awaiting the day when they could "show" the Supreme Court by closing down all our schools. It would, of course, be a simple matter to establish in the public mind that it was the Supreme Court, and not the governor and legislature, that had destroyed public education in Fulton County.

In my opinion, lawsuits in Federal court were the only remedy we might have. HOPE could provide the parties and the money to wage the legal battle that would have to come.

But the leadership of HOPE felt otherwise. There is something in the make-up of Americans that leads them to organize, sometimes for the sole purpose of organizing. So it was with HOPE. They set about on grandiose plans to create a chapter in every one of Georgia's 159 counties —"from Rabun Gap to Tybee Light," in the standard phrase of Georgia politicians. We failed. I think we had one group at Athens, the seat of the University of Georgia, and another abortive effort in Savannah, Georgia's second largest city. A young reporter in that city had corralled a number of public-school patrons and announced a public meeting to discuss the future of education in Georgia. Their speaker had canceled out, and I was prevailed upon to take his place.

Savannah is a beautiful old town, rich in history, and in resistance to change. The meeting was held at the Jewish Community Center, and attracted about a hundred people. Because there had been no frank public discussion of realities in that city before, I was somewhat fearful over what the evening would bring. It went far better than I had hoped. The audience was polite, attentive, and responsive. The questions were genuine, seeking answers rather than stating opinions. My remarks dealt exclusively with the legal aspects of the issue. The Supreme Court had ruled, I said. This was the law of the land. The school-closing statutes meant exactly what they said: the closing of schools. The Supreme Court had also rejected all devices, "ingenious or ingenuous," that might be used to subvert its purpose. The law would take its course in Georgia, as it had elsewhere in the South. For a while our leaders had been telling the people that by the simple expedient of executing leases with private groups we could continue, unmolested by the Supreme Court's decision. This was simply not the case, as had been clearly held in several legal actions. Yet no one was telling the truth to the people of Georgia. That night I did not urge an end to racial discrimination, or seek to uphold the moral basis for the decision; nor did I say that something was wrong and needed to be set right. I proceeded on the strict legal basis of what the law was, and what the law meant. Even so, I may have been the first white man in Savannah to do that.

Toward the end of the evening, one gentleman rose in the back of the room and asked a question that put the entire matter in perspective. "Mr. Weltner," he said, "if the law is like you say it is, why haven't we been told this before?" That was the point. There had been a total silence on the matter throughout Georgia. The leadership at the state level was mute.

So far as I know, HOPE never caught on in Savannah. Nor, to my knowledge, did anyone pay any attention to my analysis of the matter. Nor did I ever collect my air fare for the trip, as promised.

Meanwhile, what HOPE had been predicting, in our feeble and hesitant way, was rapidly coming to pass. I am convinced that the school system of Atlanta was saved by a last-minute development that changed the site of battle from the state's biggest and politically most insignificant city to the hallowed halls of the University of Georgia.

Being "for" the University is one of the articles of faith of state politicians. In itself, that is a worthy aim. But probably more important is the memory of the stunning political upset won by Governor Ellis Arnall when the University had lost its accreditation under the former governor. In Georgia it doesn't pay to fool around with the University.

While the Atlanta school litigation was wearying its way to final decree, Hamilton Holmes and Charlayne Hunter, two Negro high-school graduates, applied for admission to the University. They were rejected. Court proceedings followed and, with amazing speed, school authorities were ordered to admit them without delay.

34

Suddenly the situation had changed. The school-closing laws applied to all public educational facilities in the state. Yet, no one had thought that anyone other than Atlantans would ever be affected—and of course Atlantans didn't count. Now, under the law, the governor was obliged to close down the University. In fact, if he failed to do so, he could be convicted of a felony. The matter was, to say the least, critical.

Of course, Governor Vandiver did what had to be done. In a dramatic night session he went before the Georgia legislature and urged repeal of the massive resistance package. The legislature obliged. The students were admitted.

Later, the press was to lampoon the governor, all in good humor, about his "No, not one" pledge. His response, they claimed, was to acknowledge that he had, indeed, said, "No, not one." However, at *no* time during his campaign had he ever said, "No, not *two!*"

The main struggle was over. Atlanta would now follow a fairly predictable pattern, which was bound to end in the submission of a plan for desegregating its facilities, with ample time for adjustment on the part of the public to a new fact of life.

The school crisis had been met and resolved. The city of Atlanta, and the state of Georgia, had bowed to law, backed by superior power. And no one—certainly not I— discussed the question of whether it was *wrong* for a state systematically to discriminate against some of its own citizens on the basis of race. We had simply not come that far.

It was as one of the school board members said during the litigation: "You don't pay a note before it's due."

❖   ❖   ❖

Following our near miss in the County Unit case and our near tragedy in the school crisis, came the elections of 1960. It was at that point that I became interested in Democratic Party affairs, or what I hoped could become Democratic Party affairs.

The Democratic Party in Georgia is the property of whoever happens to be governor at the time. The governor appoints the state Democratic Executive Committee. The Committee sets rules for the holding of Democratic primaries, doing, of course, the governor's bidding. National Committee members are appointed by the governor. In a Presidential year, the party is active or dormant, all depending upon the governor. Long tradition holds that all national party matters must go through the state party. There was no rank and file activity of Democrats, no means of participating in party matters or party decisions. A Democrat who did not adhere to the views of the governor in office had very little opportunity of being a Democrat.

There is a delightful lady in Atlanta named Margaret MacDougall, who has been on the right side of almost every issue I can remember, and usually the losing side. She is part of what the County Unit politicians used to call "the same old crowd." In January of 1960, my wife chanced upon her at the state capitol. "Tell Charles that we are meeting tonight to get the Democrats together," she said.

The meeting, attended by more of "the same old crowd," was spent in deploring the state of affairs generally and the politicians specifically. Before it was over, I had been designated as chairman of a committee to draft bylaws for a new Democratic organization. They chose me because I was a lawyer, and lawyers are always pressed into drafting bylaws, and because I was not one of "the same old crowd." Then, too, I was available.

That night I began politics in earnest. Like most lawyers, I had thought of "some day" going into politics. The catalyst, however, was a trip to Washington on law business a few weeks later. Like millions of Americans before me, I gazed down in wonder upon the floors of the House of Representatives and the Senate. I marveled at the casual attitude of the famous men who made the laws. In the Senate, I watched in admiration as a powerful Senator strolled through the chamber door, surveyed the scene, scratched his stomach, and, utterly disregarding the speaker, walked over to join a colleague. I came home determined to convert our same old crowd into a political force.

We called it the "Democratic Forum," and our stated task was to work for the election of Democratic nominees. Soon after the organization was announced, and I had been selected as chairman, we met to consider our course. Someone raised the question, "What about Negroes?" It was a bombshell, and we agonized over it for the remainder of the evening. We could easily see our infant group scuttled by a blast in the papers calling us "race mixers." We feared, and with substantial justification, that any course which might raise the race issue would work to the detriment of our efforts. It was an easy conclusion to reach. We were trying to help elect a President and a Vice-President. If we were rejected by the community, then we would have no real force to offer to our party and to our candidates. Hence, it might be wise to proceed in the traditional way, and hope that someone else would make an appropriate effort to influence Negro citizens.

None of us had any personal objection to Negro participation. It wasn't what *we* thought. It was what others might think.

But we finally came to the conclusion that a Democratic organization should be democratic, and that we would welcome any Democrat who wished to join. It was not an easy decision. We made it and crossed our fingers.

Soon thereafter, I called upon the treasurer of the state Democratic Party to explain our purpose, and brought our organization to the attention of others within the state structure. It was no surprise that no one paid us any mind. After all, we were still the same old crowd, and, living in Fulton County and Atlanta, could not be trusted. Besides, they didn't have to count our votes.

Initially, the state Democratic leaders exhibited no enthusiasm for a national ticket headed by a young, up-East Catholic liberal from Harvard. We tried to ascertain the campaign plans of the state party, and to accommodate our efforts to theirs. But we found only that there were no plans.

Hence we made our own. We opened a large office downtown. There followed the usual frantic efforts to find and distribute bumper stickers, pamphlets, and other paraphernalia. Like any campaign headquarters, we experienced the usual personality clashes, the usual hurt feelings, and the usual difficulties in paying the telephone bill. All in all, we had a great time.

During the 1960 campaign, I learned first-hand the toils of the race question in politics. Our small cadre of hopefuls had assembled an "Advisory Committee" that included two Negroes. However, there was little or no communication between our group and Democratic efforts within the Negro community. Truthfully, there was not much need at that time. We did not know how to politick there, and Negro Democratic leaders did not relish anyone else moving in. It worked out very well, except when we came to our fund-raising dinner.

The state Democratic Party had just finished a big $100 dinner. Some of the money went to Washington. Most of it stayed home. None of it went to help our efforts, which at that time were growing in outreach and expense. Sara Craig, our ablest and most devoted campaigner, hit upon a splendid idea—a Poor Man's $100 Dinner—for $2.98 a plate. The menu was frankfurters, baked beans, light bread, and potato chips. Tickets were sold to the general public. Then the question came: "What if some colored folks show up?" Again—it was not that we had any objection to Negroes attending the dinner. The problem was that same agonizing problem faced by almost every politician down South. What effect will an *integrated* dinner have upon the campaign? There was nothing we could do but hope that no incident would occur—or, if it did, that none would be reported in the papers.

The night came, and with it the poor Democrats—all white. The bean supper was a $1,000 success.

When Election Day arrived, we carried our county by 3,000 votes. Out in the state, the margins were overwhelmingly Democratic.

That campaign taught me a lot. It was my first personal contact with established politicians. I learned something about organizing a campaign, and seeing it through. I

39

learned something about the complexities of human nature, the craving for recognition, the desire to "belong." I witnessed that strange phenomenon of devotion to cause, which impels the most unexpected people to give long and arduous hours in selfless work. And I learned something of the labyrinthine and tortuous ways of biracial politics. It was a valuable and worthwhile effort, and the friends I made then have been friends ever since.

*　　*　　*

Now I had caught the political fever, and it was inevitable that I would become involved in the 1961 mayoral campaign. That year the city primary, which is a nonpartisan election, was a free-for-all, with five candidates. Ivan Allen, Jr., an exceptionally capable business leader, was the probable front runner. Lester Maddox, a noted segregationist who had made an unsuccessful but frightening bid for the office four years earlier, was a close second. Three others were also running—a state senator, Muggsy Smith, who had long cherished the hope of being mayor, and the chairman of the Fulton County Board of Commissioners.

From the outset, the course of the campaign was set by Ivan Allen's attack upon Lester Maddox. It was a shrewd move. It narrowed the issues. It drew a line between the "good" and the "bad"—for both sides. It served to exclude the other candidates from participating—except in one vital field, the Negro vote.

Voter registration in Atlanta is one-third Negro. Allen needed these votes to win against a vocal segregationist. Smith, who had stuck his neck out long ago, felt he had some call on the Negro leadership (as indeed he had), and a mighty struggle ensued between the two. However, most of the leaders in the Negro community were behind Allen.

I placed myself in the service of Ivan Allen. In the early part of the campaign, the race issue was played down. Not many people knew what was going on, or of the fierce struggle for the support of the Negroes. All the candidates expressed the same hopes for Atlanta—to be bigger, better, and richer. Maddox played down his racial views, and tried to be just another businessman offering his services to the people. His support was already solid.

When the votes were counted, Ivan Allen was ahead, but without a majority, placing him in a runover with Maddox. Allen's strategy had worked amazingly well. He received 60 per cent of the Negro vote. Smith got 30 per cent, and the remaining 10 per cent went to State Senator Brown.

Then came the runover, which I now know from experience is the deadliest chore in a politician's life. The first returns had shown conclusively where Allen's strength lay —in the Negro boxes and in the upper-income white areas. Maddox now quickly changed his strategy to one of race-baiting and bigotry. His only hope was to so stir the passion of the people that they would turn to him. His efforts ripped the city into two camps, generating animosities that outlasted that campaign.

Three nights before the final vote, Allen asked me to appear for him at a meeting of the "Southwest Civic Council." The location was a parking lot behind an independent grocery store. A few days earlier, a Negro student leader had undertaken to picket the supermarket, alleging unfair hiring practices. A passer-by had thrown something on the youth, which he claimed was acid. It soon became apparent that the Southwest Civic Council was a Maddox organization, created solely in the interest of his campaign. The crowd, vehemently pro-Maddox, began to arrive. Except for me, almost everyone wore a Maddox button or cap. Lester arrived, to a great accolade, and delivered a thinly disguised racist appeal. It then came my turn. The master of ceremonies introduced me by name, and announced that I was speaking for Ivan Allen. At that point, a chorus of boos went up that lasted throughout my speech. "Where's Allen?" someone demanded. And someone answered, "Down with the niggers!" It was a pretty hopeless task, but I spoke out my time, solely for the purpose of speaking out my time. It was a stressful event. But, as in so many situations where harsh feelings erupt, the kinder side of human nature showed through. As I came down from the platform, a slight girl, in her early twenties, smiled shyly and said, "They're pretty rude, aren't they?" As one then unaccustomed to the rough and tumble of stomp-down politics, I keenly appreciated her friendliness.

Ivan Allen won a great victory that year, and he has become a great mayor. Nineteen sixty-one was a good year for Atlanta.

*   *   *

During that year, I had left my firm and opened a law office in partnership with Edward W. Branan, the most brilliant political analyst I know. Ed Branan was blessed with a mind that recalls dates, charts, percentages, and ratios. He also had a keen insight into the motivations and desires of people, individually and as an electorate. He had followed a parallel course in law and politics, and we joined forces in the 1960 campaign. Now we formed Weltner & Branan, purportedly for the practice of law, but primarily for the practice of politics.

During 1961, I edged closer and almost irretrievably into the 1962 Congressional contest. The race problem had been very much in evidence during the mayoralty race, but that had been Allen's problem, not mine. Then, in a minor way, it became my problem, too. I was minding my own business at home one evening when the telephone rang. It was a lawyer with the American Civil Liberties Union in New York. Someone had given him my name as a Georgia lawyer who might be willing to help in the Preston Cobb case.

At that time, the Cobb case was not a *cause célèbre.* I had a hazy recollection of it from newspaper articles, but apparently it had created a bigger stir outside Georgia than within it. Preston Cobb was a Negro who lived with his widowed mother in Jasper County, Georgia. One evening he went to the home of a white man with whom he had had some disagreement. That night the man was shot dead. The grand jury indicted Cobb. The jury convicted him. The judge sentenced him to die in the electric chair. No one of these elements is particularly unique in rural Georgia. The one thing different in the Cobb case was Preston Cobb. At the time he was sentenced to die, he was fifteen years old.

The idea of electrocuting a fifteen-year-old boy was abhorrent to many people. A concerned group was trying to find a lawyer who could file a motion for a new trial. Cobb's court-appointed counsel was reluctant to proceed further in the case. Time for filing the motion would expire in a few days, and, without the motion, the sentence would be carried out, and a fifteen-year-old boy would die.

It was an unhappy situation. Any lawyer for Preston Cobb would have to raise the issue of systematic exclusion of Negroes from juries in Jasper County. That would brand him as a civil rights lawyer and, worse still, an integrator. Being a potential candidate for Congress, there was nothing I needed less than the Preston Cobb case.

Reluctantly, I promised the lawyer I would look into the matter the next day. I arrived at the square in Monticello, the county seat of Jasper County, at ten in the morning, and made my way to the office of the lawyer who had defended Cobb. With the appropriate apologies for inquiring into his case, I asked him to relate the details of the matter. There wasn't much to it. A man had been shot to death. The boy was accused of the murder. Afterward, I went across the square to the courthouse to look at the records. They were all in order. The evidence was there. The jury verdict was there. The death sentence was mandatory.

What could be done? Nothing except to raise the issue of systematic exclusion. Driving back to Atlanta, I reflected upon my misfortune in being at home on the night of the telephone call. The vaunted ethics of the legal profession, in which I take pride, had finally caught me. If I were the only agency to stand between this outcast Negro boy and the death chamber, then like it or not, that was what I would have to do.

With a slight sense of martyrdom, I came home to find another call from the lawyer in New York. "It's all right," he said. "We've got someone who is anxious to take the case. The motion will be filed." I was off the hook. The race problem had come my way, paused briefly, and then moved on.

I have thought about the Cobb case often since then. Lawyers develop, probably of necessity, a professional detachment from the life and blood situations they encounter. I did not know Preston Cobb, or whether or not he was guilty. I did not go to Jasper County because I could not bear the prospect of a fifteen-year-old child being put to death in an electric chair, or on account of the bedrock injustice of excluding all members of his race from the jury panel. I went because a citizen was about to die without appeal unless the proper legal papers were filed at the proper place. He needed a lawyer to do this.

The townspeople thought nothing much of it. One of them told me that it wasn't nearly so bad as some said, because Preston Cobb was probably not fifteen as he claimed, but sixteen.

*   *   *

I believe that I am the only person who ever became a candidate for public office without the urging of thousands of his friends. Nobody wanted me to run, much less urged me to. My father thought it was folly. My contemporaries at the bar weren't interested. My wife was philosophically resigned. My clients, such as I had, were silent. But the urge to run can easily rationalize all those factors, as well as a total absence of financing. On December 27, 1961, ten days after my thirty-fourth birthday, I summoned members of the press (who, surprisingly enough, appeared) and announced for Congress. From that moment through the next 10½ months, I gave my all to the campaign.

I started out with my old enemy and chief villain, the County Unit System. I recounted the two instances in the past where the people had defeated the incumbent Congressman, but the Unit System had, in turn, defeated the people. It was a great issue. It combined logic and justice with the disgust and frustration of the people. The Unit System was indefensible, and the incumbent could not afford even so much as to deny my charges.

It was a pretty good campaign, although very few people had ever heard of me. Interest slowly increased, and contributions kept pace with a slim budget. But there was a force at work more powerful than the efforts I could muster—the Supreme Court of the United States.

We had lost the last County Unit case in the Supreme Court, in 1958, by five votes to four. Since then, one of the five Justices who had voted against us had left, and a new man had joined the Court. Now the Court had before it a case, *Baker* v. *Carr*, which charged that the legislature of Tennessee was malapportioned, effectively disfranchising urban voters. Finally, in the spring of 1962, the Court held the Tennessee legislature unconstitutional as charged.

At eleven o'clock that same morning, Morris Abram filed his last suit against the Georgia County Unit System. This time there was no agonizing delay. A three-judge panel was convened. It met promptly, heard the evidence, and retired for deliberation. And on a Saturday in May, I hurried away from a union hall fish fry to hear the decision announced. The County Unit System was abolished.

That ruling changed the character of a state. It made and shattered political fortunes. It elected a governor. And it put me in the Congress.

After sixteen years of losing, Morris Abram had won. He won for himself lasting credit. He won for his state a new and better day. And he won for the "same old crowd" what they so desperately desired—the right to vote.

The death of the Unit System gave our campaign new vigor and new respectability—and an outside chance to win. For the first time, people began to take us seriously. The campaign rolled on through the summer, and was helped by an astounding number of loyal and devoted people.

It is strange that politics begets its own set of friends. When I first began, I thought surely that many companions from grammar-school and high-school days would sign on and lend a hand. Not so. Political friends are born with the campaign, and I can count on one hand the number of long-time friends who made substantial contributions, in either time or money.

Looking back at the people who *did* help, I cannot understand what motivated them. None of my supporters hoped for patronage, or personal power, or tangible returns. Few, if any, had ever worked in politics before. Few had known me before the campaign began. Yet they came, and they gave, and because of them I won. They know how much I owe them.

The primary was on September 13. As the first returns came in, I trailed by 4,000 votes. With no idea of which boxes were in, we could only imagine that the matter was hopelessly lost. Then, about ten o'clock, we were roused from the sink of despond by a television announcer, who said, "There has been a dramatic change in the Fifth District Congressional race. Challenger Charles Weltner is now leading the incumbent Congressman Davis!" As it turned out, I kept the lead, but two other candidates in the race sliced off enough of the vote to throw me and Mr. Davis into a runover.

I have noted the trials of runovers. I had received 77,000 votes, but how in the world could we ever get all those people back to the polls? Where could we possibly find the money to campaign for two more weeks? How could we get our campaign workers to stay with us that long?

There was one problem in particular. In the first primary, I had benefited from great interest in the other races that were run simultaneously, particularly the primary contest for governor between former Governor Marvin Griffin, a hard-line segregationist, and State Senator Carl Sanders, a moderate. A mighty effort had been mounted in the Negro community to defeat Griffin, whose cure for the South's accelerating racial difficulties was the judicious use of the "blackjack sapling." But now Sanders had won. The only other contest requiring a runover was the race for lieutenant governor, in which only Lester Maddox (the same Lester Maddox) and another hard-liner were left. That race did not generate much interest among my supporters. In particular, Negroes found nothing of interest in either man.

But somehow we got another campaign going. There was more television, more handshaking, more telephone calling, and more radio ads—based on what proved to be a fairly effective appeal: "Vote again, win again." Among the Negro community, 90 per cent of whom had voted for me, there were more appeals to "go back and finish the job."

The second primary campaign that year ended, according to an old Atlanta tradition, in an Election Eve rally at the Wheat Street Baptist Church, a large Negro congregation in the heart of Atlanta.

In the first city primary the previous year, that church had been the scene of feverish activity by the contending Ivan Allen and Muggsy Smith camps. On that Election Eve there had been several dozen candidates, with their claques, to swell the crowd. Even the seats in the choir loft had been filled. After the speaking, rival groups of supporters had lined the narrow street and produced an impromptu demonstration that combined a samba line with jazz cadence. It was an unforgettable sight.

Now, a year later, we came back to Wheat Street. Notices had been sent out calling on all citizens to attend the meeting. Invitations had been extended from pulpits. And the grapevine that operates in the Negro community had been signaling all to come. At eight o'clock, Ed Branan and I arrived. The church, not counting the balconies and choir loft, was less than half filled. The crowd, if it could be called that, was subdued. We were depressed. The meeting was opened by the pastor of the church, Dr. William Holmes Borders, a big man with a fine, resonant voice. The next speaker was Warren Cochrane, the head of the Negro YMCA. Cochrane did his best to stir the crowd, and made the best case for me that my want of experience and attainment could provide. Then the patriarch of the community, the late Judge A. T. Walden, spoke. Occasionally one of the speakers would generate a response, but only occasionally. Clearly, the people were weary of politics and politicians.

The memory of that meeting is still vivid. It was a dreary scene compared to Election Eve of the mayoralty race the previous year. There were no banners, no snake lines, no shouting cohorts, no cheers, just a church half-filled with tired people who had come because someone had asked them to. They were older people, patient with years of grinding poverty and disappointment. I watched them as the others spoke. They had heard all this before. Some politician was going into office to make a better life for them, to "raise them up," to "cast off the shackles of yesteryear." They had already voted for me once. Two weeks ago, these same men and women had taken half a day to ride the bus, lose pay, arrange for their children, and go to the polls—and wait—and vote. And now they were being asked to do it again.

Like any other candidate, I wanted to win, and I knew that I could not win without a solid turnout of my supporters. I could not win without these people in that church, and thousands more like them. If it was too much trouble for them to get to the polling places the next day, if the weather was bad, if any one of a hundred things came up—I was lost. I don't remember what Borders or Cochrane or Walden said that night. I don't remember what I said. But I remember what I thought as I looked out over the faces in that church. If I win, I thought, I will not forget these tired and trusting people. If I win, I'm going to do *something* to help them.

The next day it rained. It started at daylight and kept up into the early afternoon. Then at three o'clock the sun came out. When the votes were counted, I had 75,000; Mr. Davis had 63,000.

I won that primary election because I worked hard, and because a lot of friends worked hard. I won because I drew well throughout the white sections of the district, and had solid support among Negroes.

But the fact is that I did not so much win, as my opponent lost. He had totally cut himself off from that 20 per cent of his constituency that was Negro. His appreciation of the problems of the Negro in America had changed not one iota in the past fifty years. It was, therefore, unnecessary for me to make any commitments or to incur any obligations—or, indeed, even to express my views on the race question—in order to attract Negro support, which I welcomed. Mr. Davis never mentioned race throughout the campaign. In all fairness, I must say his campaign was open and aboveboard. But times had changed, and he had not.

For me, the race issue, even during so prolonged and vigorous a campaign, was postponed to another day.

Now, as the Democratic nominee, I undertook the third campaign of that year. My Republican opponent moved in to attack, and I was on the defensive. The Republicans had two campaigns. The one waged in the Negro community sought to lay upon me all the sins of the Georgia Democratic Party, including the County Unit System, along with the imperfections of noted Southern Democratic governors who preached a racist doctrine. The Republican campaign in the white community was waged against John F. Kennedy and both his brothers, with a heavy flavor of racism.

A few days' observation of the enthusiasm and vigor of the Republican campaign made the exhaustion of my own supporters, physically, mentally, and financially, apparent. Two reactions were especially frightening. The first:

"Well, you won the nomination and you've got it made. What are you worrying about?" The second: "I voted for you, and I know you'll make a good Congressman. Now, I believe in the two-party system, you know, and, although it won't really matter, I'm going to vote Republican." Sometimes they would even add, "Of course, you are the better man, but, after all, I *do* believe in the two-party system."

The prospect of being the instrument of electing the first Republican Congressman from Georgia in ninety years was appalling.

But somehow, we dug in, and held on, and won.

*   *   *

There were many memorable incidents in that third 1962 campaign.

Practically every civic club in Atlanta invited the two candidates to debate before them that fall. There were breakfast meetings, dinner meetings, and supper meetings. And there were meetings in the Negro community. One of these was at the Butler Street YMCA, and featured a debate between the candidates, with questions from the audience. We spoke, then answered the usual inquiries, generating nothing new and little different. Then a man who had taken a violent personal dislike to me (as was his right) and made that known by publications scattered throughout the community, rose and in a most belligerent tone demanded, "I'd like for Mr. Weltner just to tell me what he thinks about segregation. Just tell me, right now."

The room hushed in expectation. No one had ever asked me that question. It was sort of an unwritten rule not to ask it. The importance of my answer was quite plain. The meeting was attended by a large number of influential Negro leaders. My opponent's supporters were there in force, to make whatever capital they could of my answer, wherever they could. A reporter for the Negro daily, which was opposing me, was present. It was a critical moment.

I responded, "Are you asking that question of *both* candidates?"

"No, just of you," he shouted back.

There was a murmur of disapproval and a few voices called out, "Both candidates!" I turned to my adversary, and he nodded that he, too, would respond to the question.

I began: "I believe in the law of the land. The Supreme Court decision is the law. Therefore, all publicly financed or publicly supported facilities and institutions must be offered to all members of the public alike. The law forbids discrimination, and I support the law. There are areas outside of the scope of the law. Social relationships should be determined by private individuals, and one should be permitted to associate with whomever he pleases."

I sat down to await my opponent's response, but he failed to join issue. The chairman arose and declared the meeting adjourned. The audience relaxed, a bit disappointed, and I relaxed, vastly relieved.

Once again, my answer had bespoken the precepts of the law. Those of the conscience remained unspoken.

2

The years of man are threescore and ten. At exactly midpoint in my years, a new life began for me and my family. We rented our home in Atlanta, packed up our worldly goods, collected our children's health and school records, loaded our belongings in a rented trailer, and, with a giant English sheep dog, began our journey to Washington.

Surely since the beginning of our Republic, new Members of Congress have experienced the same apprehension and timidity, and have shared the same expectations and hope. There, in Congress, is the seat of power. There decisions are made. There the course of history is plotted. There the affairs of nations are settled. There mankind rises or falls. There is the capital of the world. There is power for those who can command it. There is fame for those who can capture it. There is accomplishment for those who can serve. There is failure, defeat, and even dishonor, for those whose stars are crossed.

Some men come to spend one term and then recede into the great mass of mankind. Some stay a lifetime, generating little more than a ripple on the surface of events. Some are catapulted into history. Where would my road lead? One term, then back to the law practice? Forty years, then anonymity? Or would it be something more?

Every new man must ask himself these questions as he enters the Chamber for the first time, stands to take his first oath of office, and then, sinking into his seat, looks about him at the awesome place of decision.

Washington was both better and worse than my wife and I had expected. Old friends—Ed Branan, Sara Craig, Rosa Lee Cook, and Greg Favre—came with us to staff the office. We found new friends among Members of Congress, at our new church, and in our new neighborhood. It is a pleasant city, and there are many opportunities for all ages.

As with most new Members, the mail was an absolute dictator for at least six months of the first year. Representing the second largest Congressional District in the nation was a high privilege, but the volume of mail was commensurate with its size. That, and the total lack of Capitol Hill experience of our staff, combined to demand a twelve-hour day for many months. But time is a good teacher. Soon we learned what had to be learned, and did what had to be done. Soon we found new ways of seeking out our constituents, and offering the services that a well-run Congressional office can provide.

The issues of the 1962 election, such as they were, had been Federal aid to education and medical care for the aged. The race question had not been an issue, nor did it seem to be much on the public mind or conscience until mid-1963. Certainly, no one came to the 88th Congress prepared for the tumultuous events of that biennium—least of all me.

President Kennedy prepared messages on Administration measures, and we received them. Bills were introduced and referred to committees. There was little significant action of any kind in the 88th Congress for the first three months, a delay dictated by an uncertain Democratic majority. Somewhere along in March of 1963, the President sent us his first message on civil rights. Its major thrust was in the area of voting. There were also some provisions for technical assistance to school districts that might undergo difficulties in complying with court orders for desegregation. In retrospect, there was nothing in it to arouse the populace or to upset even the most ardent segregationist.

I was on the floor when the message was read. A few minutes later, a page called me to the telephone room to take a call from Ed Branan. My law partner and campaign manager had come to Washington as head of the staff, a position known on Capitol Hill as "Administrative Assistant." It was always difficult for me to think of him by that title, for he was still a partner. His call was to advise me that the very astute Washington correspondent for the *Atlanta Journal,* Margaret Shannon, had called to ask my position on the President's Civil Rights Bill.

Finally, it looked as though the race problem would catch up with me. So far I had eluded it all my life. During all three of the 1962 campaigns it had been muted, by both my opponents and me. Events had not forced me to take a public position on oft-discussed but never passed civil rights measures. But finally, it appeared the matter could no longer be avoided. Margaret Shannon knows the ways and the wiles of the politician. On anything of any substance, she would persevere until she found her answer. Then she would print it.

I prepared a statement which said simply that I hoped everyone would let everyone else vote, without the need for new Federal laws. But Miss Shannon never called back. The question at that point was of such small importance that it wasn't worth a second call.

Once again the issue had passed me by.

But that was in March. Two months later the nation was turned upside down, and I, along with every other conscious Southerner, was caught in the maelstrom.

In the spring of 1963, new Negro protest demonstrations erupted over the South. Atlanta had its share. But the center of activity, and the center of passions, was in Birmingham. That city gave to the world unforgettable pictures of police dogs attacking colored children, men and women driven by cattle prods, crowds bowled over by the force of fire hoses. What happened in Birmingham was reported around the world in seconds. As the demonstrations, and the official resistance, continued, the nation's anger was aroused. The intransigence of the city authorities, the belligerence of the governor of Alabama, the violence with which citizens were subdued, combined to create an atmosphere of crisis.

I well remember what one of my Georgia colleagues had to say about the matter: "You hear all this talk from these Southern boys about Kennedy. Well, you can talk all you want to about that. When they sic police dogs on little children, something's going to happen. That just isn't right."

He was right, of course. The public makes short shrift of debating points and fine distinctions, and pays little heed to details of legislation when its daily fare consists of fresh reports and pictures of police dogs, cattle prods, and fire hoses. All the explanations and words in the world cannot erase the force and impact of those photographs.

What was done there was plainly wrong and the public demanded a remedy.

Quite naturally, the nation, and the world, looked to Washington for action. The initial cause for the demonstrations had been the refusal of proprietors of public facilities to admit Negroes. The sit-in tactic, fashioned three years earlier in Greensboro, North Carolina, had come to full fruition in Birmingham. The Administration sought to eliminate the cause of the controversy by proposing that places of public accommodation be required to extend their services without regard to race or color. On the evening of June 11, the nation watched as President Kennedy submitted this historic proposal to the American people. The reaction was overwhelming. The first word I received from home was a telegram shrieking, "Save us from this mad dog tyranny." Other telegrams followed. There were telephone calls. Then the letters began to flow in. The country talked of little else. The demonstrations in Birmingham had succeeded in placing the issue inescapably before us. The race problem had come full force to Congress in the same year that I had come. It was no longer to be avoided, or ignored, or overlooked.

On the day following the President's television address, the House took up the bill to extend and expand the Area Redevelopment Administration. This program was designed to build up the economies of depressed areas by developing new payrolls and new economic activity. Its prior history had not been characterized by outstanding success, but it appeared to most that it was worth at least further trial. The ARA Bill had come out of my committee —Banking and Currency. It was opposed by Republicans, although its precursor, the Depressed Areas Program, had been an Eisenhower measure. Shortly before the bill came to the floor, the Administrator of ARA had promulgated a set of regulations designed to eliminate racial discrimination in facilities constructed under the program. The opposition, seizing upon the distress of Southerners, made this the focal point of their argument. After hours of heated debate, the roll was called. The bill failed by five votes, 204 to 209.

The failure of that measure was directly attributable to the President's message of the preceding night. I know, because I heard three Members state that they had planned to support the bill, but would now oppose it because of the President's civil rights speech. These three votes cast the other way would have provided the margin of victory. One of the "knee-jerk" conservatives from the other side of the aisle (now a former Member, after serving one term) approached me with the question, "Are you boys going to send a message to the White House today?" Thus ARA went down, the first Congressional victim of resistance that set in as a reaction to the race issue.

When the President's Civil Rights Bill was drafted and presented to the Congress, I was, of course, asked my position, and this time I did not escape. I placed the following statement in the *Congressional Record*:

> The Supreme Court decision of 1954 is still the law of the land. It is the law, and it will remain the law. Accordingly, we must recognize that all governmental, or publicly supported or controlled facilities must be made available to all citizens. . . . The 14th and 15th Amendments, forged in the bloodshed of a century ago, are [also] the law of the land. Their guarantees must extend to every citizen. Nor can there be any justification for withholding or denying any of the

rights there secured on grounds of race or color. Particularly, the right to vote must be extended to all persons, without regard to color, who can qualify under fairly administered standards. Those who seek, by harassment, subterfuge, or intimidation, to deny the ballot to others do nothing but invite Federally supervised voting procedures. Unless justice is done at the courthouse, it will be done at the Capitol. . . .

There remains the question of fair play on the part of privately owned facilities serving the public. Is it fair that some Americans are admitted, and others turned away? Is it fair that some Americans are welcomed on one side of a store, and rejected on the other? If we seek fair play, then we must acknowledge that it is lacking here. [But] is the remedy found in a public accommodations law of nation-wide application? . . . I think not. I do not think that prudence dictates such a mandatory rule as the national public accommodations proposal, and I cannot support it. . . . Our nation can overcome its problems—but we must solve them, not ignore them. Long-term solutions are still to be found, not in hastily passed statutes, but in a full and fair opportunity for every American to attend a good school, to earn a good income, and to achieve full development of his own talents and abilities. . . .

Comment ranged from those who were horrified that I recognized the Fourteenth Amendment as anything other than an abolitionist hoax, to the Negro minister who vowed that he would spend the next eighteen months in assuring my defeat. "You are determined to keep me in slavery," he shouted. These were, of course, the extremes. My statement probably reflected the great majority of well-motivated white opinion, who found the compulsion of the public accommodations section somewhat ahead of their thinking, and somewhat counter to their concept of proprietorship. At home, most organizations which memorialized upon the subject took an opposition stance. This was true initially of both Atlanta daily newspapers. The Chamber of Commerce resolved against the section, but at the same time urged its member businesses to lower racial barriers. Substantially the same action was taken by the hotel and restaurant associations. Thus a position opposing the mandatory provisions of the law, but urging the goals sought by that law on a voluntary basis, was probably representative of the District for which I spoke.

All that was in June. Talk around the Capitol forecast passage of the Civil Rights Bill in October, based on House action within six weeks, with maybe ten weeks in the Senate. It was on that timetable that the March on Washington was scheduled. Surely, the civil rights leaders thought, the Senate will be long into a filibuster by the end of August. Thus the coordinating committee of the civil rights groups chose August 28 as the date for the Washington March for Jobs and Freedom.

Beginning in July, the March became the major topic of conversation on Capitol Hill. It was discussed in offices, in the corridors, and in the cloakroom. It was the major, primary, and dominant subject of comment and speculation.

On August 27, everyone made plans for the following day. Truthfully, no one knew what it would bring. Some offices granted a holiday. Shoppers postponed their plans. Downtown Washington was avoided. One Southern Member was so apprehensive of the morrow that he spent an uncomfortable night on his office couch. Our office was at that time—and still is—so concerned with getting out the mail that we could ill afford to lose a day.

My usual route to work was down Massachusetts Avenue to the Rock Creek Parkway, thence past the Lincoln Memorial to Independence Avenue, then on to Capitol Hill and the Old House Office Building. That morning I kept a sharp eye out for the demonstrators. All I saw was policemen. The town was deserted. There was no traffic, not even the usual careening, speeding cars, jockeying for position along the parkway. There was only open space and the police, three deep at each significant intersection. Along the Mall were movable comfort stations. There were tents with red crosses, for those who might be overcome while overcoming. Washington that morning had a strange aura of quiet and expectation.

There was an important measure on the floor that day, but the main interest was the March. Would it be peaceful? Or violent? Would it succeed? Or fail? Someone brought a portable television set into the cloakroom. Many Members, mostly Southerners, crowded in to watch the proceedings.

The main address of the occasion was delivered by my former constituent, the Reverend Martin Luther King. Thousands will remember that speech—"I have a dream." It was impressive and eloquent, and it cut through to the most hard-bitten. One Member from North Carolina ventured that the whole affair would have been vastly improved if Dr. King alone had addressed the assembled multitude. Finally, another of my constituents, Dr. Benjamin Mays, offered the benediction: "And help the weary travelers to overcome someday soon." It was a moving event. Men and women, young and old, white and black, had come from across the entire nation to demonstrate their hopes and beliefs. When it was concluded, the cloakroom was silent. No one scoffed. No one laughed. It was as though all of us began to sense that there was something to what we had heard for so many months.

There must be countless incidents connected with that historic day. Surely, every one of the two hundred thousand took home memories and impressions that will last a lifetime. I know one Southerner who went out, not to march, but to watch. As he watched, there came trudging by a young lady he had known back home. She had come in on the bus, and was returning that night. Consequently, she was obliged to carry with her the small bag containing her traveling articles and lunch. What could a Southern gentleman do? Nothing but carry her bag, and, in so doing, join the March.

* * *

A few weeks after the March on Washington, while the Congressional committees were still grinding away at the civil rights legislation before them, another incident blazed into the conscience of the nation.

On September 15, 1963, four small Negro children went to Sunday school in Birmingham and were in the midst of their lessons when a sudden explosion took their lives. The bombers had done their work well, and timed the device to explode at an hour when Christians would be at worship.

Early that day, the news of this senseless tragedy flashed across the nation. Ministers, North and South, discussed the murders from their pulpits. Our own pastor devoted his entire sermon to the evil incident.

Surely, I thought, there would be an immediate reaction on the floor of Congress. Surely some Southerner would speak on the subject. But Monday came, and except for one mention of the bombing by a Northern Senator, there was silence in Congress.

I decided that I should speak. On the following noon, September 17, these brief remarks were entered in the *Record*:

> Mr. Speaker, there was a time when a Southerner was "moderate" for what he did not say. There was a time when silence amid the denunciations of others was a positive virtue. But, in the face of the events of Sunday, who can remain silent?
>
> Those responsible for the deed in Birmingham chose a Sabbath morning as the time, a House of God as the place, and the worshipers within as the victims. I do not know what twisted and tortured minds fashioned this deed. But I know why it happened. It happened because those chosen to lead have failed to lead. Those whose task it is to speak have stood mute. And in so doing, we have permitted the voice of the South to preach defiance and disorder. We have stood by, leaving the field to reckless and violent men.
>
> For all our handwringing and headshaking, we will never put down violence until we can raise a higher standard. Though honest men may differ as to means, can we not affirm as a great goal of this Republic the concept—equality of opportunity? Mr. Speaker, we need not so much new paragraphs on books of the law, as new precepts in the hearts of men. We need to raise, and to follow, this standard —as old as Christianity and as simple as truth—"Let right be done."

There was nothing remarkable about my statement. I had stated my own thoughts on the matter of Southern leadership, and the good or evil that is dependent upon the quality of that leadership. It was a fairly simple proposition: that in the United States we do not bomb churches and murder Sunday school children.

But some were intensely agitated by the very suggestion that something could be wrong with any Southern state, particularly Alabama. There followed cries of "Judas," "Benedict Arnold," and the other epithets of treason. Over all, however, the response from home was overwhelmingly approving of what I had said, and of the fact that I had spoken.

The reaction of the Northern press also amazed me. Day by day, reporters from Northern papers came by the office to talk to me—why, I could not understand. Their impressions of the South and of Southerners apparently came from *Uncle Tom's Cabin,* and within this framework of misunderstanding, they were shocked that a Southerner had the temerity to come out against church bombings.

I suppose that the Birmingham statement branded me as "soft on segregation." With it, I incurred the permanent alienation and hostility of a substantial number of "No, not one" types, in Georgia, and across the South.

*   *   *

It will be recalled that the March on Washington was scheduled to coincide with a Senate filibuster. In August, the House Judiciary Committee was still far from ready to report out a Civil Rights Bill. A perverse situation had arisen to confound the supporters of the bill. On the Judiciary Committee were several Southerners who were dead set against a bill in any form. At the opposite end of the spectrum was a group of liberals who were determined to

66

pass out more than President Kennedy had sent in. In the middle was a third element, those who wished to see some bill reported out and sent up to the floor. For a while, there was a peculiar coalition of Southerners and liberals, both supporting a vastly strengthened and more comprehensive bill, but for exactly opposite reasons—the liberals because they wanted it passed, and the Southerners because they thought it would be easier to defeat.

The Administration realized they were about to be closed in a box, and so the Attorney General was sent up to soothe the liberals and work out a compromise. Finally the deadlock was resolved, and in November the committee reported out a moderate bill, consisting of the Administration proposal plus a Fair Employment Practices provision and a section providing for cutting off Federal funds from state and local agencies that practiced racial discrimination. This measure was then sent to the Rules Committee, presided over by the bellwether of Southern conservatism, the venerable Howard Smith of Virginia.

A few days later, President Kennedy went to Dallas. There, Lyndon B. Johnson became the first Southerner in a century to occupy the office of President of the United States.

So many words have been written of President Kennedy's assassination that there is little anyone can now add. It was a profound shock for every sensate person. All of us felt some of the guilt for that tragic day. All of us had, in some measure, remained silent while strident voices were abroad. All of us had failed to do, or say, some of the things that needed doing and saying.

For a time the nation mourned its young chieftain. Then, in the way of the world, it turned again to its daily tasks. The President was dead. Now, there was another President, a man who, for three years, had been far from the forefront of public consciousness. Soon those who are mindful of such things would begin to discern and to define the "Johnson style," vastly different from that of his predecessor.

On December 23, Congress was still in session, and the President invited the Members of Congress to a White House reception, partly to compensate for disrupting so many well-laid Christmas plans. It happened that at the time the President joined the assembly, I was talking with Secretary of State Dean Rusk, a fellow Georgian. Thus, we went through the line together. Mr. Rusk was kind enough to introduce me to the President, and observed that I was *his* Congressman. The President didn't hear him. A few minutes later, the Speaker of the House was engaged in conversation with Mr. Johnson, and seeing me standing near by, hailed me over. "Mr. President," he began, "this is one of the new Members from Georgia, Mr. —." At that same instant, the President called across the room to one of his Texas friends. Two introductions having failed to make a dent—one from the Secretary of State and one from the Speaker of the House—I resigned myself to remaining forever outside the circle of Presidential intimates. The following day, the House concluded its business.

With barely pause enough to observe Christmas, the House went back into session in January 1964. Now there was scarcely interest in anything other than H.R. 7152, the Civil Rights Bill.

On January 31, 1964, the House passed the motion to consider H.R. 7152, resolved itself into the Committee of the Whole House on the State of the Union, and the issue was joined. On most bills, the debating time is divided equally between the majority and minority, with the committee chairman and ranking opposition member controlling the time. In this case, however, the time was divided into three parts, and parceled out to the majority, controlled by Mr. Celler of New York, chairman of the Judiciary Committee, Mr. McCulloch of Ohio, the ranking Republican member, and Mr. Willis of Louisiana, speaking for the committee opponents, all Southerners. For several days before, there had been meetings of Southern Members to plot the strategy of the opposition. Judge Smith was the clearly recognized leader of the caucus. I attended none of the sessions, and cannot vouch for what transpired. But the head count on the bill was of such magnitude that its certain passage must have been a depressing incubus upon the proceedings. The question was not whether some civil rights bill would pass the House, but what amendments might be added, and what changes might come in the Senate, where unlimited debate had in the past worked far-reaching modifications upon similar measures.

The general debate provided in the rule consumed two days, and then we began the process known as "reading the bill for amendments under the five-minute rule." Any Member may seek recognition for the purpose of offering an amendment to any paragraph which is being read by the clerk. He is allowed five minutes to speak on behalf of his proposal. Thereafter any other Member may speak for five minutes, for or against the amendment. Debate on any pending amendment may be concluded by majority vote of the Members present. Cloture, cutting off debate, is a frequent move in the House. Senate rules require two-thirds of the Members present to cut off debate. The greater majority required, and long tradition, have confined Senate cloture to only the rarest of circumstances. It speaks well of both sides in the House that not once during the nine long days that the House considered the Civil Rights Bill was debate terminated except by unanimous consent.

The quality of discussion was worthy of a great deliberative body. There was little rancor or bitterness, and both sides sought to keep a little humor in the proceedings. When the whole matter was concluded, the House rose in approbation of both majority and minority managers, and Southern Members stood and applauded each.

Those were long days. There were well over a hundred amendments, and I made a conscientious effort to understand and cast an intelligent vote on each. It was exceedingly difficult on many occasions. The very first amendment was directed to Title One, dealing with voting rights. It sought to prohibit within the Fifth Circuit Court of Appeals what was termed "forum shopping," meaning the seeking out of friendly judges. I voted against that amendment, while most Southerners supported it. It failed by a vote of 125 to 176. That 125 votes was the most that the Southern bloc ever mustered—a second high-water mark of the Confederacy, 100 years after Gettysburg. For anyone who had doubted, that tally was undeniable indication of the course the bill would take.

Some amendments were impossible to vote for *or* against. Judge Smith offered an addition to the public accommodations section to the effect that nothing in that title should be construed to require any person to render involuntary servitude. To vote for that proposal would equate the provision to slavery. To vote against it would evidence a predilection *toward* slavery!

Toward the end, few Members were paying close heed to the amendments that were proposed. One of my Georgia colleagues remarked that we were now betting on jockeys, not horses. He put it well. Members would rush from the cloakroom, ask whose amendment was "up," and vote for or against depending upon whether or not the author was a Southerner.

I had decided to vote against H.R. 7152, and had so advised anyone who inquired of me. On the afternoon of the final day, a young friend called me off the floor, and urged me to at least abstain if I could not vote "Yes." I explained that I never intended to abstain on any measure, certainly not on this one, and that I would vote "No." Yet he persisted, arguing that I was some sort of "spokesman" for an otherwise silent moderate white opinion throughout the South, and that I owed some consideration to this non-District constituency. I replied that my constituency was three counties in Georgia. Besides, I said, the bill would certainly pass by a two-to-one margin without my vote. "I know that. That's not the point," he said. "Somewhere along the line some Southerner has got to stand up on this issue. You have the perfect chance to do it." I told him I appreciated his interest, but could not do as he asked.

By eight o'clock that evening, time had run out and the record of debate on H.R. 7152 was completed. Because of the hour, some of us had ordered dinner at the House restaurant. Two bells rang: straight roll call. There was plenty of time to eat, and wait until the second time through the roll. The second bells rang. I left the table, and walked up the marble staircase to the Chamber.

... "Watts." "No."

"Weaver." "Aye."

"*Weltner.*" "*No.*"

The vote was cast. I turned to go.

I should have been glad it was over. The days and nights had been long, the debate wearing, and the issue itself was stale from overdiscussion and overemotion. I should have felt a sense of relief that the House might now turn its attention to other fields.

I returned to my table, and Ed Branan said, "Did you vote?" "Yes," I said. There was nothing more to say. The question had come and the vote was cast. Yet I sensed no finality about the matter. Instead, there was a vague lack somewhere, as though something were left undone that needed doing.

That was on the evening of February 10, 1964.

❖   ❖   ❖

Public life leaves little time for regret or retrospection. Hard on the heels of the first crisis on H.R. 7152 came a smashing new issue. On Monday, February 17, 1964, the Supreme Court reversed a three-judge panel of the Fifth Circuit in Atlanta in the case of *Wesberry* v. *Sanders*, and ruled that the Congressional Districts of Georgia were so malapportioned as to deprive them of the equal protection of the law. The Court said that the apportionment of the Fifth District of Georgia, my District, which contained one-fifth of the people of Georgia yet elected but one-tenth of the state's House delegation, was violative of the Constitution. My District was at that time the second

72

largest in the nation. It was twice as big as the average Congressional District, and three times the size of the smallest District in Georgia.

There followed the familiar anguished cries from the advocates of unrepresentative government. "Usurpation" . . . "reckless disregard of precedent" . . . "trampling upon the rights of states" . . . "legislating by judicial decree" . . . "amending the Constitution by court order"—the whole sequence was there. In the meantime, cooler heads became concerned with the import of that ruling. It meant that several states must now undergo redistricting, or face court-ordered elections at large. It meant that rotten boroughs in Congress would soon be a thing of the past. It meant that the House of Representatives would, at last, be representative.

The Georgia legislature was then in session, and the repercussions were clearly audible as far north as the Potomac. Georgia went through the same travail that most states suffer under similar circumstances. But because three members of our House delegation retired that year, it was possible to make the required changes without the "sudden death" alternative of placing two Members in the same District. My own District was split right down the middle, and the eastern half was designated as the Fourth District. By late spring the shouting was over, and the state was redistricted in a proper manner, with a minimum of gerrymandering.

My personal political situation was about as it had been. I still had the traditional Republican areas, a Negro population comprising one-fourth of the registered voters, and a sizable area that was rural and agricultural.

That was an exceedingly busy spring. With the first

73

shoots of green came the first shouts of politics, readying for the September primary and the November general election. And throughout it all, the Senate debated the House-passed version of the Civil Rights Bill.

There was initially an effort to pass that version as it stood. Had that been the case, it could have gone directly to the President for signing. But soon it became evident that some changes would be made in the Senate, and the House would have another vote on the bill.

Toward the end of the long debate, Senate action became clearly foreseeable. The terms of the amendments which would be offered and accepted were well known to all observers, and I began to think hesitatingly of the possibility of supporting the final version. The first person to suggest that possibility was a friend who had supported me all along. At a post-office ceremony, he said, in hushed tones, "You ought to vote for that thing up there when it comes back." Although he did not identify the measure to which he referred, his meaning was plain. He paused for a moment, then moved on.

The prospect of another vote was not a happy one. It was no great joy to vote down a measure designed to provide equal rights and equal justice to American citizens. It would be no better to vote against the modified bill that would return to the House.

By that time, almost every responsible voice in the country, outside the South, had declared for the bill. Many white Southerners had come reluctantly to the conclusion that something of that sort was essential to progress in the South. And notwithstanding the specific details of the legislation, the inspiration and goal it embodied was one which I shared.

74

And so I began to think. The prospect was somewhat frightening. It was easy to foresee what would be said of me, my loyalty, my intelligence, and my ancestry. It was easy to see what political capital might immediately result to my opponent.

When I suggested the idea to two of my friends, they were startled into speechlessness. Finally, one remarked, "Well, it would be pretty rough."

My father, who has never advised me on any vote, observed that some people prefer a stubborn dolt to a pliant saint. Quite naturally, I wondered what my colleagues would say. I wondered what those who had voted for me in the past would say—and what those who would vote that fall would say.

But the Senate debate wore on, and the time was fast approaching. My closest campaign advisers were divided on the issue. My wife was in favor of the bill, and said only that I should do what I felt was right.

Thus divided, I left Atlanta for the last time before the final vote, and returned to Washington.

By then, the Senate had voted cloture and passed the bill 81 to 19, and the House Rules Committee had voted it out. The majority was so certain that no one bothered to count heads, and there were few letters or telephone calls on the subject.

The vote would come on Thursday, July 2, on a motion to adopt the Senate amendments and pass the bill.

I suppose that I was one of the few persons in the country whose mind was not firmly made up on the measure.

My difficulty was fairly obvious. I had opposed, and still was reluctant to accept, the means adopted by the bill to secure equal rights. Yet, the goal of equal rights was something I had long ago accepted, and found in accord with my understanding of the Constitution and my basic religious beliefs. And it was the course of history.

The question was whether I could, or would, make that belief a matter of record at that time, on that bill, under those circumstances.

Over several evenings at home I had tried to write down the considerations presented by the measure. After many long hours, this was the result:

> Over four months ago, the Civil Rights Bill came to this floor. Its stated purpose, equality of opportunity for all Americans, is a proper goal. But I questioned its means, and voted against passage. Now . . . this measure returns for final consideration. . . . By the time my name is called, votes sufficient for passage will have been recorded. What, then, is the proper course? Is it to vote "No," with tradition, safety—and futility?
>
> I believe a greater cause can be served. Change, swift and certain, is upon us, and we in the South face some difficult decisions. We can offer resistance and defiance, with their harvest of strife and tumult. We can suffer continued demonstrations, with their wake of violence and disorder. Or we can acknowledge this measure as the law of the land. We can accept the verdict of the nation. Already, the responsible elements of my community are counseling this latter course. . . . I shall cast my lot with the leadership of my community. I shall cast my vote with that greater cause they serve. I will add my voice to those who seek reasoned and conciliatory adjustment to a new reality. And, finally, I would urge that we at home now move on to the unfinished task of building a new South. We must not remain forever bound to another lost cause.

The question remained whether I would dare speak what I had written.

At ten o'clock the following morning my father called me.

"I suppose the resolute has made his decision?" he asked.

"I'm going to vote for it," I said.

"You're on the side of history. I'm proud of you."

The noon bell rang and the House gathered with a sense of anticipation. Practically every Member was present. The galleries were jammed, and the press was out in full force. I asked for two minutes of the hour's debate, and was declined. But somehow Wayne Hays of Ohio learned of my intent and spoke to Ray Madden of Indiana, who controlled the time. Mr. Madden gave me one minute, and Wayne sent a note up to the Speaker, requesting for me a "long minute."

Then my Georgia colleague Carl Vinson, with fifty years in the House, came over to me. "I understand you are planning to vote for this bill?" he said. I told him that he was correct. Scowling, he offered, "Well, profiles in courage, and all that. But I hate to see you throw away a promising career." He spoke out of genuine concern for me, for which I shall forever be grateful. A few minutes later, he came back and asked: "I understand you are planning to *speak* to this bill?" "Yes, sir," I said. He fixed me with a keen eye, looking down his fierce nose. Somewhat sadly, and wonderingly, he shook his head, and moved off. Then it came my turn.

I walked to the well of the House, read my remarks, and sat down.

I remember with gratitude that one Georgia colleague who had voted against the bill came by my office an hour later to state that he found no fault with what I had done.

Two hours later we landed at the Atlanta airport. On the apron was a small group of my friends, waving campaign posters. There were also a few newsmen, who immediately asked the obvious question: "Why did you change your vote on the Civil Rights Bill?" It was a question that I had to answer hundreds of times during the next four months.

At home, my wife greeted me with mock concern, and said, "I see you made it home." Then my son Phil, ten years old, picked up the newspaper I had brought. The headline shouted, "Civil Rights Bill Passed." In smaller type it said, "Weltner Votes 'Yea.'" He read it aloud. "Daddy, did you vote for the Civil Rights Bill?" he asked. I nodded. "Good," he said.

That was his only comment—"Good." There was no question of constitutionality, of Federal intervention, of oppressive regulation, of property rights, of political repercussions, of changing votes, of inconsistency. Simply, "Good."

On the Fourth of July, two days after the vote and one day after the President had signed the law, came the annual Independence Day parade in Atlanta. I arrived at Baker Street early that afternoon to ride in an open convertible, my name printed on either side. Parades are difficult in the best of circumstances. You have to keep smiling. You have to be alert to recognize friends in the crowd, and to ignore insults. You have to take the stony and sullen silence from some of the onlookers. But this particular parade, on this particular day, was a totally unknown quantity. All over the South, in the wake of the enactment of the Civil Rights Bill, there was tension and uncertainty. People who had still cherished the hope that "it would never happen" now knew that it had happened. No one knew what their reaction would be, but I would soon find out: there were 200,000 lined up on both sides of Peachtree Street.

The reaction was surprisingly anticlimactic, and therefore heartening. Some clapped, some did not. As we turned down the crest of Peachtree toward Five Points, one man yelled, "Hey, niggerlover!" Another, farther down, shouted, "What would your granddaddy think of you now?" Some just shook their heads and shrugged their shoulders. Those who had cheered in the past did so now, only more loudly, while those who had booed did likewise. All in all, it seemed that I had generated considerable vehemence among both friends and detractors.

That night I was to play baseball at the ball park, as teammate to other politicians, against the Hollywood All Stars, who traveled a circuit to make money for charity and to make diversion for themselves.

All men have a hidden desire to be baseball stars, and I am no exception. I played first base, and was passably proud of my performance—two double plays, two put-outs at first, and one double. (I also quit after the third inning while my luck was still holding.) The double, however, was really a single, expanded by a fielding error. I even tried to make it a triple, and pounded down the third base line before I noticed a teammate standing on the sack. Desperately, I tore back to second.

Then came one of the great moments of that year. Some-one in the stands called out, in a voice that everyone could hear, "*What's the matter, Charlie? Can't you make up your mind?*"

*   *   *

The weeks that followed were not all pleasant. There were abusive letters and telephone calls. There were strained friendships. There were people who said they would never again support me. Everywhere the question was the same. And everywhere I tried to answer. Some accepted my answer; others did not.

At one political rally, an acquaintance came over to me and said, "Charlie, when you voted for that bill, were you prepared to be thrown out of office over it?" I said I was prepared for such an event. "Well, you are a nice fellow personally, and you have a lot of friends. But we are going to do everything we possibly can to see that you never go back to Congress."

Then there was a man I approached with outstretched hand at a fish fry. Putting his hand behind his back, he said, "I shook hands with you the *first* time you ran."

Then, too, there was the opposite reaction. There were gratifying occasions when strangers would come up to offer their support on the basis of my vote. One man, from whom I least expected it, said, "It's about time somebody down South stood up." And people from every social and economic stratum came into our campaign headquarters to help.

*   *   *

The four months that followed disclosed the vastly dif-fering viewpoints of people at home. There was, under-

standably, one central issue in the Congressional campaign
that fall.

Some violently disapproved of me, my voting record,
and everything connected with the Democratic Party.
Some ascribed to me unworthy motives in voting for the
Civil Rights Bill. Some viewed me with distrust, and
pointed to my second vote as clear evidence in support
of that conviction. Some were in favor of the Civil Rights
Bill, and were pleased that I had voted for it. Some disapproved of the vote, but credited me with voting my
convictions in a difficult situation. And some were *for* me,
period.

When 120,000 citizens expressed their opinions at the
polling places, all these factors were represented. After all
the speeches were made, and all the appeals concluded,
and all the fervor spent, the votes were cast.

Sixty-five thousand voted "Yes."

Fifty-five thousand voted "No."

The issue was decided.

*   *   *

That election was, of course, important to me. And I
believe that it might have had some significance beyond
a mere choice between two candidates for Congress.

As only one of 435 members of one body of the Congress, whether I returned to Washington or to the law
practice would be of slight moment to the country. There
were, and are, many men and women who might serve
equally well or better in that body.

But the usual Congressional considerations were almost
wholly subordinated in that election to a question of in-
finitely greater magnitude:

Would a Southern District seek reasoned adjustment to a new reality? Or would it seek to remain forever bound to another lost cause? In 1964, the people at home came face to face with the race issue.

In that year, the people decided.

PART TWO

3

*The Southern physical world [is] a sort of cosmic
conspiracy against reality in favor of romance. The
country is one of extravagant colors, of proliferating
foliage and bloom, of flooding yellow sunlight, and,
above all perhaps, of haze. Pale blue fogs hang above
the valleys in the morning, the atmosphere smokes
faintly at midday, and through the long slow afternoon, cloud-stacks tower from the horizon and the
earth-heat quivers upward through the iridescent air,
blurring every outline and rendering every object
vague and problematical. . . . The dominant mood
. . . is one of well-nigh drunken reverie—of a hush
that seems all the deeper for the far-away mourning
of the hounds and the far-away crying of the doves—
of such sweet and inexorable opiates as the rich odors
of hot earth and pinewood and the perfume of the
magnolia in bloom—of soft languor creeping through
the blood and mounting surely to the brain.*

—W. J. Cash

✤ The Civil Rights Act of 1964 did not "solve" the race
problem. It did not mean the end of racial injustice or
racial strife. In the summer of 1964 the nation continued
to suffer the agonies of the past.

Young Negroes threw themselves under the wheels of

police vehicles. White-robed Klansmen plotted, and accomplished, the death and dismemberment of those they deemed their enemies. White housewives, hunched over bridge tables, shook their heads in bafflement. Teen-agers waved Confederate flags in the faces of the United States marshals. Congressmen made speeches. Trolley riders explained to each other that their maids did not hold with all this, but liked things fine the way they were. Young radicals moved Negro audiences with their revolutionary appeals. The sitters-in sat in. The bloody-shirt wavers waved.

In the Presidential election, the only issue in the South was race. And, when the votes were counted, it was obvious that this issue had overcome the demonstrable success of the policies and programs of the Democratic Party, and that relative peace, a high level of prosperity, and dramatic economic growth meant less to the majority of Southerners than did the one issue of race. In Alabama, five out of six incumbent Democratic Congressmen were defeated. Georgia, the only state in the Union that had always voted Democratic, went for Goldwater by 100,000 votes. In Mississippi, a senior Congressman was unable to beat back the challenge of an unknown Neshoba County farmer. Five Southern states, along with Arizona, provided all the electoral votes the Republicans got.

The question must be asked: *Why* did all this happen? *Why* was it necessary for the most advanced nation the world has ever seen to undergo such torment over an issue supposedly settled a century past? *Why* was the principle of equality for all men, clearly enunciated in the Declaration of Independence, still the subject of uncompromising antagonism almost two hundred years later?

The answer is not simple, and it is not to be found in the present, or even in the present century. For Southerners, even more than for most people, it is as William Faulkner wrote—"The past is not dead. It is not even past." Southerners share a common thread of thought, with their present generation and with those of the past. My time is different from that of my father, and his from my grandfather's. Yet there is an identity that spans decades and classes and generations and communities throughout the South. And no one who does not know the Southern past can hope to answer the question of *why*.

The history of the race issue in American politics is the history of opportunities lost and lessons unlearned. Time and again our fathers were confronted with the problem, and turned away. Time and again they deferred solutions to another day. The strife of the present is the legacy of that postponement. And if we would know *why*, we must track the story to its headwaters, then follow down its course.

* * *

The South began, as did the nation, when three English ships with 144 souls landed on the bank of the James River on April 26, 1607. Twelve years later, twenty-seven colonists met in a little church to form the first legislative assembly in the New World. They elected a Speaker, a Clerk, and a Sergeant at Arms. Six days later they adjourned because the weather was so hot that it caused "alteration of the health of the divers present."

In August of that same year, a strange craft moved up the tide toward the dock at Jamestown. She was short and thick, with high bow and stern, looking like a half-moon on the waters of the bay. Canvas billowed about her, and the stubby snouts of cannon protruded from her bulk-heads. It was the Dutch man-o'-war *Jesus*. She was more than just another ship from the Old World, containing more than just another cargo for the colonists. For aboard the *Jesus* were, according to the diary of John Rolfe, "20 negars." These hapless souls had been captured from a Portuguese slaver, and were to be the first slaves in the English colonies. That day began an evil which besets us still.

And thus, ironically, the first beginnings of the democratic institution of representative government in the New World, and the first beginnings of the peculiar institution of slavery, occurred in the same season of the same year, at the same place.

These twenty slaves were the first. Thereafter, their numbers grew slowly. By 1700, there were only 25,000 in all the colonies. But a great increase came after 1713, when Britain won rights in Africa—and began to traffic in that continent's most profitable commodity, human beings. Within two years, there were 60,000 slaves. By 1760, they numbered 400,000. Slaves equaled the free population in Virginia, and outnumbered whites 70,000 to 30,000 in South Carolina. Three-quarters of them were found in Maryland and the Southern colonies.

Slavery was a Southern institution, but slaving was a Northern activity, headquartered in Newport, Boston, and Salem, and later New York City. Leaving Boston with a cargo of rum, slavers crossed the Atlantic to West Africa, where the rum was bartered for slaves. The human cargo was then transported to the West Indies, where it was sold for sugar and molasses. The slaves stayed in the Indies until they became accustomed to the American climate, then they were sent north and sold to the colonists. Meanwhile, the sugar and molasses went back to New England, where they were converted into rum, and the cycle began again. A successful trip would earn the slaver 300 pounds. The business was fairly stable. A healthy male would bring 21 pounds, a female 18, a child 14. One 60-ton ship could hold 75 slaves, crammed "'tweendecks," a space about 3 feet high. The trade was profitable to Northerners, many of whom would forget that it was Yankee ingenuity that spread the peculiar institution.

Though the North provided the supply, the South made the demand. New England was a land of small farms and rocky soil, and its people turned to manufacturing, shipping, and trade. These pursuits better fitted the semitrained laborers from Northern Europe than blacks straight from Africa. The South was suited for agriculture, and soon developed the plantation system. Here, on the great stretches of fertile soil, was plenty of work for black hands. Hence, the North became commercial and free, the South, agrarian and slave.

Georgia at first forbade the introduction of rum and slaves—it had been initially founded by James Oglethorpe as a debtor colony, and the Trustees likely felt the first citizens were too poor to afford either commodity. The rule could hardly have been based on moral grounds, because Oglethorpe himself was manager of the Royal African Company, the greatest of the English slave-trading corporations. The prohibition placed Georgia on a different footing from her neighbors. Without slaves, agriculture could exist only on small holdings, and small planters could not compete with the plantations of South Carolina. At one point all but 500 persons removed from the colony.

Yet, men being as they are, ways were soon discovered to avoid the Trustees' proscription. In 1739 planters began to "hire" Negroes from South Carolina slaveholders for hundred-year terms, with payment of "rental" in advance. Finally, under pressure, the Trustees lifted the restriction in 1750, and Georgia joined her sister colonies in buying and selling human beings. The colony prospered in the mainstream of the slave economy. By 1760, Georgia had 6,000 whites and 3,000 blacks. Thirty years later there were 53,000 whites and 29,000 slaves.

      ❖   ❖   ❖

From August of 1619 until the Constitutional Convention in 1787, slavery grew and prospered along with the nation. There was little opposition to the institution on moral grounds, though some felt that Africans were so inferior that they should not be admitted under any circumstances. The English Quakers in the middle colonies were outspoken opponents. But slavery drew support from many clerics, particularly within the Methodist Church. George Whitfield, one of the founders of Methodism, wrote:

"It is plain that hot countries cannot be cultivated without Negroes. What a flourishing Georgia might have been had the use of them been permitted years ago. . . . I should think myself highly favored if I could purchase a good number of them in order to make their lives comfortable, and lay a foundation for breeding up their posterity in the nurture and admonition of the Lord."

John Wesley, however, disagreed, characterizing slavery as "that execrable sum of all villainies," and pleaded:

"Alas for those whose lives were here vilely cast away

through oppression, through diverse plagues and troubles!
How long wilt Thou hide Thy blood! How long wilt Thou
cover Thy slain!"

Yet there was no general moral condemnation of slavery. It was viewed as economic necessity to the South, and
economic opportunity to the North. The people, unaroused
and unchallenged by public and religious leaders, gave it
little thought. Indeed, there seems to have been no real
debate on the subject for well over a century and a half,
until the summer of 1787, when delegates met in Philadelphia to consider their General Government, and determine what should be done.

A major controversy soon arose over legislative representation. Virginia, being a large state, sought representation on the basis of population, including three-fifths of
the slaves. New Jersey, a small state, proposed equal representation for all states. It fell to Connecticut to offer
the scheme that was ultimately adopted: a bicameral
legislature, with one house based upon population and the
other upon state equality.

In this struggle the Negro was but a pawn. He figured,
not as a human being, but as three-fifths of a human being.
This fraction had first been applied under the Confederation in calculating the tax burden of each state: the
Revenue Act of 1783 required states to pay taxes propor-
tionate to their population, with three-fifths of slaves
counted. Being property, slaves indicated ability to pay.
At Philadelphia, both the Virginia and New Jersey plans
used the fraction, one for legislative representation and
the other for revenue assessment. The Connecticut compromise continued it in fixing membership of the House
of Representatives, after an amendment by Pinckney of

South Carolina, proposing that slaves be counted equally, was rejected by a vote of 8 to 2. The three-fifths fraction itself was not the heart of the issue. It was nothing new, having been in effect under the Articles of Confederation, and was part of all three major proposals. Rufus King later stated: "This rule was adopted because it was the language of America." Equal status for Negroes was rejected overwhelmingly when it was considered, but even then the struggle was not for Negro equality, but for state power. It was a fight between big states and small states, not free states and slave states.

Slavery itself became an issue at a later stage in the proceedings, when Luther Martin of Maryland moved that taxes on the importation of slaves not be forbidden. Only North and South Carolina and Georgia, among Southern colonies, still permitted this duty. Martin declared that slavery had weakened the states, and that its increase would lead to insurrection. He described the institution as "inconsistent with the principles of the Revolution," and said it was "dishonorable to the American character to have such a feature in our Constitution." His charge did not go unanswered. John Rutledge of South Carolina, described as a "fine, fierce, hawk-eyed, white-haired gentleman of the old school," responded with contempt that he did not fear revolt, and added, "Religion and humanity have nothing to do with this question. Interest alone is the governing principle of Nations. The true question at present is whether the Southern states shall be parties to the Union."

Rutledge's colleagues from South Carolina, the Pinckneys, supported him. This exchange precipitated a crucial battle, and one that almost prevented Union. Massachusetts had already abolished slavery. The Continental Congress, through the Northwest Ordinance, had forbidden slavery in the Northwest Territory, which was to become the states of Ohio, Indiana, Illinois, Michigan, and Wisconsin. Because of their economies, Georgia and the Carolinas were convinced that without slavery they faced certain ruin. Georgia's economic experience during the days of slave prohibition lent fuel to these fears.

George Mason of Virginia, an ardent advocate of personal liberty, evidenced the contradiction within many Southerners. Himself a slave owner, he spoke against the institution. He blamed Britain for foisting upon the colonies "this infernal trade," and for her efforts in blocking any attempt to halt it. New England did not escape his censure, for he reminded his listeners, "Some of our Eastern brethren embarked in this nefarious traffic." Speaking of the institution itself, he continued: "Every master of slaves is a born tyrant. They bring the judgment of Heaven on the country. As Nations cannot be rewarded or punished in the next world, they must be in this. By an inevitable chain of causes and effects, Providence punishes national sins by national calamities." How did Mason reconcile his strong feelings against the "infernal trade" with his own slaveholdings? There was no need to, and he made no attempt to. The necessity was obvious.

As is the wont of every assembly, the Convention referred the slavery problem to a committee for resolution. The committee's report was a compromise, again, in this form:

> The Migration or Importation of such Persons as any of the States now existing shall think proper to admit, shall not be prohibited by the Congress prior to the Year 1800,

but a Tax or duty may be imposed on such Importation, not exceeding ten dollars for each Person.

The year 1800 was extended to 1808, and the provision was adopted by a vote of 7 to 4, with New Jersey, Pennsylvania, Delaware, and Virginia voting against. The trading states of the East voted for the compromise out of fear of some future regulation similar to the English Navigation Acts. Then, too, they were reaping rich dividends from the trade. Ellsworth of Connecticut favored letting every state import what it pleased: "The morality or wisdom of slaves are considerations belonging to the states themselves. What enriches a part, enriches the whole, and the states are the best judges of their particular interest."

Back home, General Pinckney explained the Northerners' position on slavery in urging ratification: "Show some period when it may be in our power to put a stop, if we please, to the importation of this weakness, and we will endeavor, for your convenience, to restrain the religious and political prejudices of our people on this subject. In short, we have made the best terms for the security of this species of property it was in our power to make. We would have made better if we could, but on the whole I do not think them bad."

Thus the crisis was passed, and the compromise concluded. Without it, it is possible that Georgia and South Carolina would have rejected the Union. Ellsworth observed, probably correctly, "This widening of opinions has a threatening aspect. If we do not agree on a middle and moderate ground I am afraid we should lose two states. With such other as may be disposed to stand aloof, we should fly into a variety of shapes and directions, and most probably into several confederations, and not without bloodshed."

The fugitive slave provision drew fire from some opponents, as well. Delegates asked why human property should have to be delivered at public expense any more than a horse that had strayed. However, the final form was adopted unanimously. Like the three-fifths clause and the clause on slave trading quoted above, the fugitive slave provision does not once use the word "slave" or "slavery":

> No *Person* held to *Service or Labor* in one State under the Laws thereof, escaping into another, shall, in Consequence of any Law or Regulation therein, be discharged from such *Service or Labor,* but shall be delivered up on Claim of the Party to whom such *Service or Labor* may be due. [Emphasis added.]

Luther Martin, who first opened that Pandora's box, commented on this phraseology in a speech before the Maryland Assembly:

"They anxiously sought to avoid the admission of expressions which might be odious to the ears of Americans, though they were willing to admit into their system those things which the expressions signified."

Here was the first of many lost opportunities. At the Convention, for the first time, there was a forum, and a body of men empowered to act for the whole of the new nation. Since 1619 slavery had been a part of the New World. Men had sold and bartered other men. They had traded children like they traded heifers and lambs. The conscience of some had been aroused from time to time over the preceding decades. Yet, the Negro appeared at the Convention not as a citizen, nor as an American, nor as the creature of a benign God, nor as a human being. From the first, he was reckoned only as a piece of property, and only three-fifths of a piece of property at that. It was not *his* status that concerned the delegates, but that of his owners. The North, fearing the political power that large numbers of Southern slaves might bestow upon their masters, cut him down to three-fifths. The South, fearing the North but unable to impose its full will, acceded.

When the question of slavery itself arose, a solution was postponed. Some, like Martin, thought slavery evil, and would have abolished it. Others, like Rutledge, thought it beneficent to the poor benighted savage, and profitable to the white—in sum, a positive good. Still others, like Mason, saw it as tyranny, yet "essential." Mason's view prevailed. The convention did not prohibit further importation of slaves then and there, but only prospectively as of 1808. Nor did it, even for that date, abolish the institution, but only the importation of new slaves. Though most of the drafters disapproved of slavery, they provided no solution, only compromise. The problem was reserved for some other day and some other generation. Yet it was not in truth a compromise, only postponement.

It is quite true that the delegates had not come to Philadelphia to discuss slavery alone. The status of the Negro was not nearly so important to them as the status of the thirteen colonies, and the relationships they would forge among themselves and with the General Government. But the question of slavery, and of the Negro, did arise, and it could have been settled in Philadelphia.

That opportunity was lost. The issue would be settled at a later time, not in peace, but in blood.

*   *   *

Had the thirteen colonies comprised all the potential territory of the United States, the slavery question might have subsided with the passage of time. The states had struck a balance of power between agrarian and commercial interests, and between slave and free. It was a balance that each group guarded jealously.

But the vast reach of new lands to the west, in the course of things, were opened up, and their inhabitants petitioned for statehood. With each settlement that arose on the prairies and along the rivers, the issue was rekindled. North feared South, and South feared North. Each feared the harm that decisive power in the hands of the other might work upon its own interests. And each was determined, at all costs, to prevent hegemony by the other.

In 1819, a bill was introduced in the Congress for the admission of the Missouri Territory as a new state. The new constitution of the Territory legalized slavery on a permanent basis. Thus the issue was joined, and the lines were drawn.

The prospect of a new slave state held terrors far beyond its own admission. The Northwest Ordinance of 1787 had barred the institution from all states that would be created from the Northwest Territory. The admission of Missouri would break the line that had been there established, and serve as precedent for other new slave states from the Louisiana Territory. Each side saw the fate

97

of Missouri as its own. If she were slave, the South and
its economy would stand. If she were free, the South would
soon be outnumbered in the Congress, and Southerners
feared their economy would be destroyed.

Northern moderates sought to solve the dilemma by
the gradual elimination of slaves in Missouri, proposing
that all children of slaves born in the Territory become
free at the age of twenty-five. The House passed the proposal, but it met a deadlock in the Senate, which was
equally divided between slave and free states.

A compromise was offered by Henry Clay. Missouri
would be admitted as a slave state, as that was already
her character. But to preserve the balance in the Senate,
Maine was to come in as a free state. Slavery was to be
forever barred from all territory north of 36 degrees 30
minutes latitude, that being the present northern bound-
ary of Arkansas.

It is not difficult to imagine the feelings that were engendered during debate on this momentous issue. Northerners taunted their Southern brethren with seeking to
establish new markets for the flesh and blood of men
"raised like black cattle and horses on the plantation."
Indignant Southerners replied with threats of secession
and war. Howell Cobb of Georgia shouted, "You are kin-
dling a fire which all the waters of the ocean cannot ex-
tinguish. It can be extinguished only in blood!" Jefferson,
now at Monticello, wrote to Congressman John Holmes of
the Maine district of Massachusetts:

> But this momentous question, like a fire-bell in the night,
> awakened and filled me with terror. I considered it at once
> as the knell of the Union. It is hushed, indeed, for the
> moment. But this is a reprieve only, not a final sentence. A

geographical line, coinciding with a marked principle, moral
and political, once conceived and held up to the angry passions of men, will never be obliterated; and every new irri-
tation will mark it deeper and deeper. . . . But as it is, we
have the wolf by the ears, and we can neither hold him, nor
safely let him go. Justice is in one scale, and self-preservation
in the other.

John Randolph of Virginia became so agitated that for
days he could eat nothing but gruel and crackers. Always
impetuous, he called for immediate secession.

Finally, Clay's motion carried. For a while, but for a
while only, as Jefferson had observed, the balance was
maintained. There were now twelve states free, and twelve
states slave. Thus the Union had been saved in its severest
crisis since the Constitution.

But sectional differences, supposedly settled by the
Compromise, continued to smolder beneath the surface.
The temper of the nation reached its boiling point eight
years later when the commercial interests of the North
pushed through Congress the Act of 1828, known as the
"Tariff of Abominations," which was considered a severe
discrimination against Southern interests. The controversy
it engendered brought the Union once again to the brink
of civil war.

It was South Carolina, in a desperate search for some
defense against the tariff, that invoked the doctrine of
Nullification, as it was to be exhumed again in 1954 against
the Supreme Court's prohibition of school segregation.
The Nullification argument said that one state, as a separate member of the Federal Union, could declare a Federal law to be null and void within its own jurisdiction.
Jefferson had so counseled during the fight against the

Alien and Sedition Acts, and Virginia and Kentucky had so resolved. Now South Carolina took up the old refrain, declared the Tariff of 1828 void, and threatened to put an end to collections at the port of Charleston. John C. Calhoun, the power behind resistance, was Vice-President, and had no voice in the Senate. Therefore, floor action was led by South Carolina's Senator Robert Young Hayne. On January 21, 1830, the Senate heard these words from Hayne:

> Sir, as to the doctrine that the Federal Government is the exclusive judge of the extent, as well as the limitations of its powers, it seems to me to be utterly subversive of the sovereignty and independence of the States. It makes but little difference, in my estimation, whether Congress or the Supreme Court are invested with this power. If the Federal Government, in all or any of its departments, is to prescribe the limits of its own authority, and the States are bound to submit to the decision, and are not to be allowed to examine and decide for themselves, when the barriers of the Constitution shall be overleaped, this is practically "a government without limitation of powers." The States are at once reduced to mere petty corporations, and the people are entirely at your mercy.

Five days later Massachusetts' Senator Daniel Webster replied, in one of history's great orations:

> Whence is this supposed right of the States derived? . . . We are here to administer a constitution emanating immediately from the people, and trusted by them to our administration. It is not the creature of the State Governments. . . . The people, then, sir, erected this Government. They gave

it a constitution; and in that constitution they have enumer-
ated the powers which they bestow on it. They have made
it a limited Government. They have defined its authority.
. . . They have left it with the Government itself, in its
appropriate branches. Sir, the very chief end, the main
design for which the whole constitution was framed and
adopted, was to establish a Government that should not be
obliged to act through State agency, or depend on State
opinion and discretion. The people had had quite enough
of that kind of government, under the confederacy. . . .
Congress could only recommend; their acts were not of bind-
ing force till the States had adopted and sanctioned them.
Are we in that condition still? Are we yet at the mercy of
State discretion and State construction? Sir, if we are, then
vain will be our attempt to maintain the constitution under
which we sit.

Webster's eloquence had no effect upon the inflamed
passions of South Carolina. Calhoun continued to resist
the tariff. President Jackson, himself a man of no small
determination, was equally adamant that the laws of Congress be enforced. The whole question became one not of
taxes, but of regional animosities. Beneath the furor, the
issue of slavery, muted for a time, lay festering.

In 1830, Calhoun and Jackson met at a dinner party,
and there ensued a scene that thrilled the nation. The
dinner was under way, and the guests had already heard
a long string of toasts when the President was called upon.
He rose, and, looking straight at Calhoun, said in a com-
manding voice: "Our Union: It must be preserved!"
Abruptly the clatter of conversation and glasses ceased.
Everyone stood for the toast. Calhoun's hand was shaking

so that the wine ran down the side of his glass. In a hesitating tone, he responded: "The Union, next to our liberty most dear. May we all remember that it can only be preserved by respecting the rights of the States and by distributing equally the benefits and burdens of the Union."

While the tariff controversy continued, the abolitionists were not deterred from their ways. William Lloyd Garrison of Boston founded his paper, *The Liberator*, in 1831. Garrison rejected gradualism and, in the sentiments of latter-day crusaders, demanded "Freedom Now." The first issue of his paper disclosed the ardor of his views:

> I am aware, that many object to the severity of my language; but is there not cause for severity? I *will* be as harsh as truth, and as uncompromising as justice. On this subject, I do not wish to think, or speak, or write, with moderation. No! No! Tell a man whose house is on fire, to give a moderate alarm; tell him to moderately rescue his wife from the hands of the ravisher; tell the mother to gradually extricate her babe from the fire into which it has fallen;—but urge me not to use moderation in a cause like the present. I am in earnest—I will not equivocate—I will not excuse—I will not retreat a single inch—AND I WILL BE HEARD. . . .

In 1832, South Carolina finally did as she had threatened, and passed the Ordinance of Nullification. Her resolve was firmly stated:

> [We] do further Declare that we will not submit to the application of force on the part of the Federal Government, to reduce this State to obedience, but that we will consider the passage, by Congress, of any act . . . to coerce the State, shut up her ports, destroy or harass her commerce, or

to enforce the acts hereby declared to be null and void, otherwise than through the civil tribunals of the country, as inconsistent with the longer continuance of South Carolina in the Union: and that the people of this State will thenceforth hold themselves absolved from all further obligation to maintain or preserve their political connexion with the people of the other States, and will forthwith proceed to organize a separate Government, and do all other acts and things which sovereign and independent States may of right to do.

Now the move fell squarely to the President. Jackson prepared to march against South Carolina with 35,000 troops, himself in the lead. Calhoun, who had resigned the Vice-Presidency to return to the Senate, was the particular object of his wrath, and the President announced that Calhoun would be tried for treason, and, if convicted, hanged "high as Haman."

Once again, the lines were drawn. Once again the old differences of North and South, commerce and agriculture, free and slave, brought the Union to the abyss. And once again it was Henry Clay who developed an accommodation of the warring factions, and worked out a program under which the tariff was lowered and South Carolina finally repealed her ordinance. A second great crisis had passed, but not without bitterness that endured throughout the lives of the principals. Jackson, late in life, declared his only regret was that he had not shot Henry Clay and hanged John Calhoun.

Nor were the scars of the Nullification controversy limited to the great figures of history. South Carolina stood for the South, slave and agrarian, in durance vile to a

Federal power considered oppressive and bent upon her destruction. Economic interest, sectional loyalties, revulsion over abolitionist tactics, fears of Negro domination, and a keen sense of oppression and exploitation by outsiders made their firm imprint on Southern minds during that bitter strife. What followed did little to stay the sprouting seeds of disunion.

The struggle between free and slave states emerged again during the period of the Mexican War. President Polk was accused by Northern Whigs of mounting against Mexico a "monstrous, guilty and oppressive crime." As enemies of slavery, they considered it a "bloody Southern junket to steal territory and to find bigger pens to cram with slaves." Corwin of Ohio compared Polk to Tamerlane sitting on a throne of 70,000 skulls. "If I were a Mexican," he shouted, "I would tell you: 'Have you no room in your country to bury your dead men? If you come into mine we will greet you with bloody hands, and welcome you to hospitable graves!'" Intense feelings split the Whigs along sectional lines, into "Cotton Whigs" and "Conscience Whigs."

Nor did the successful prosecution of the war by Polk salve the wounds that had been reopened. Representative David Wilmot of Pennsylvania offered an amendment to an appropriations bill for the peace settlement with Mexico which would have prohibited slavery in any Territory acquired from the defeated nation. Again the issue came to the floor of Congress. The House adopted the Wilmot Proviso, but it failed of passage in an equally divided Senate. The South argued that all Territories were the property of the people of the states, and that they should enjoy them equally; that to permit Northerners to transport their property into Territories, and to prohibit Southerners doing the same, was an act of invidious discrimination and a denial of the equal protection of the laws.

Thus the Wilmot Proviso became the new symbol of an ancient struggle. Three times it passed the House of Representatives, and three times it met stalemate in the Senate.

Yet, Senate inaction could not forever stave off the resolution of the conflict. By 1850, California had taken matters into her own hands, formed a provisional government, adopted a constitution which forbade slavery, and petitioned to enter the Union. If the new state were admitted, the existing balance would be destroyed, with the immediate prospect of Congressional action against slavery.

Southern states declared their intention to resist admission to any extremity. For the third time Henry Clay arose to offer compromise, this to be his last. California, being in fact free, would be admitted as free. New Mexico and Utah would be formed into Territories without prohibition of slavery. Slave trade, but not slaveholding, would be abolished in the District of Columbia. Finally, a new and more stringent Fugitive Slave Law would be passed for the protection of Southern interests. Five of Clay's bills were passed, and became known collectively as the Compromise of 1850.

The debate brought to the floor of the Senate the brightest stars in its long history—Webster, Clay, Calhoun, Seward, Chase, Jefferson Davis, and Stephen Douglas. The great speech of the occasion was Webster's, in support of the Compromise.

> I wish to speak to-day, not as a Massachusetts man, nor as a northern man, but as an American, and a member of the Senate of the United States. . . . I speak to-day for the preservation of the Union. "Hear me for my cause." . . .

New England roundly condemned him as an "apostate," a "falling star," "Lucifer descending from heaven." Walt Whitman made him the subject of his poem "Ichabod." The speech cost Webster his political life. Yet, it was what he deemed necessary to preserve the dearest object of his heart, the Union.

Calhoun violently opposed the Compromise. Old and close to death, he sat in the Senate, huddled in flannel robes, too weak to talk, while Mason of Virginia read his speech. Calhoun saw the portent of the North's expanding population, and declared it necessary that Congress reverse the trend and recover "equilibrium" for the two sections. He even suggested that the executive power be divided between two Presidents, one from the North and one from the South. Slavery was a positive good to him. He wrote:

> There never existed a civilized society in which one portion of the community did not, in fact, live on the labor of the other. Better, then, to have inferior blacks labor in paternalistic slavery for Southern whites than to imitate the factory "wage slavery" of the North with its capital-labor strife and seasonal starvation.

Nor did he accept the doctrine of equality:

> Nothing can be more false than the opinion that all men are born free and equal, for it rests upon the assumption of a fact which is contrary to universal observation.

His arguments have been repeated and refined by generations of Southerners.

Death came to the old man a few weeks after the Compromise. His last words were: "The South, the poor South."

Four years later, a group of dissident Northern Whigs, abolitionists, and free-soilers formed a pro-Union, anti-slavery party. Thirty Congressmen declared themselves for "free soil, free speech, free labor and free men." They called themselves after Jefferson's first faction, Republicans.

That same year, Stephen Douglas introduced his Kansas-Nebraska resolution. Acting from a variety of causes, including his personal interest in a transcontinental railway, Douglas proposed to divide the Nebraska Territory, which was north of the Missouri Compromise line, hence free, into the Territories of Kansas and Nebraska. Each Territory, when it came into the Union as a state, would make its own choice as to whether it would be slave or free. Douglas himself, a moderate in this instance, declared that he cared not whether slavery be voted up or down. His proposal pleased neither side. The North objected to the possible introduction of slavery into free soil. The South objected to "popular" or "squatter sovereignty," as it was called.

Despite inflamed opposition from both extremes, Douglas' bill became law. Bitter exchanges marked the debate. At one point, Senator George Badger of North Carolina complained that he could not take his "old black mammy" to Nebraska if the people of the Territory forbade it. He loved his old black mammy, he said, and she loved him. Turning to Senator Benjamin Wade of Ohio, he asked:

"Surely you will not prevent me from taking my old black mammy with me?"

"It's not that he cannot take his old black mammy with him that troubles the mind of the Senator," sneered Wade, "but that if we make the Territories free, he cannot sell the old black mammy when he gets her there."

Kansas became the scene of bloody conflict under the popular sovereignty plan. Both sides sent in settlers in an effort to control the way the state would vote. "Border Ruffians," armed with bowie knives and revolvers, according to Northern papers, rode across from Missouri on Election Day, took charge of Kansas polls, barred free-soil men from voting, then rode home again.

The North countered by sending in colonies of tough abolitionists with rifles paid for by church collections. Small-scale civil war flamed. The free-soil town of Lawrence was burned by Missourians, and John Brown dragged five proslavery settlers from their cabins on Pottawatomie Creek, and butchered them and their families in cold blood.

The agonies of "Bleeding Kansas" found their echoes in Congress. In the Senate, Charles Sumner of Massachusetts, a violent foe of the Kansas-Nebraska Act, condemned it as "The Crime Against Kansas":

> Sir, the Nebraska Bill was in every respect a swindle. It was a swindle of the North by the South. On the part of those who had already completely enjoyed their share of the Missouri Compromise, it was a swindle of those whose share was yet absolutely untouched. . . . It was a swindle of a broad territory, thus cheated of protection against Slavery. It was a swindle of a great cause, early espoused by Washington, Franklin, and Jefferson, surrounded by the

best fathers of the Republic. Sir, it was a swindle of God-given inalienable rights. Turn it over; look at it on all sides, and it is everywhere a swindle; and if the word I now employ has not the authority of classical usage, it has, on this occasion, the indubitable authority of fitness. No other word will adequately express the mingled meanness and wickedness of the cheat.

In the course of his speech, Sumner accused the elderly Senator Butler of South Carolina of "taking the harlot, slavery, as his mistress." Enraged at Sumner's diatribe against the South and against his uncle, Representative Preston Brooks of South Carolina walked into the Senate chamber two days later and administered a prolonged and severe caning to Sumner. Caught behind his desk, the Senator could not escape. Douglas and Toombs of Georgia stood by while Brooks continued to shower blows upon the Northerner with a gutta-percha cane. Finally, wresting his desk from its moorings, Sumner fell to the floor upon his back.

The reaction to the Sumner-Brooks incident was electric. It was in itself a man-to-man civil war. Sumner, disabled for three years, was re-elected, though physically unable to sit. Overnight Brooks became a hero to the South. The people responded by showering him with gifts of canes.

The battle over slavery and free soil had been waged in varying degrees of fervor since 1787, with the Executive, the Congress, and the electorate all participants. One element had remained silent, however—the Supreme Court. That silence was broken in 1857, when Chief Justice Roger B. Taney delivered his opinion in the case of *Dred Scott v. Sandford.*

The case itself was turned aside on a simple technical point. Scott, a slave, was not a citizen, therefore he had no right to plead in the courts of the land. Yet the Court went much further than this:

> Now . . . the right of property in a slave is distinctly and expressly affirmed in the Constitution. The right to traffic in it, like an ordinary article of merchandise and property, was guaranteed to the citizens of the United States, in every State that might desire it, for twenty years. And the Government in express terms is pledged to protect it in all future time if the slave escapes from his owner. . . . And no word can be found in the Constitution which gives Congress a greater power over slave property, or which entitles property of that kind to less protection than property of any other description. The only power conferred is the power coupled with the duty of guarding and protecting the owner in his rights.

> Upon these considerations, it is the opinion of the court that the Act of Congress [the Missouri Compromise] which prohibited a citizen from holding and owning property of this kind in the territory of the United States north of the line therein mentioned, is not warranted by the Constitution, and is therefore void; and that neither Dred Scott himself, nor any of his family, were made free by being carried into this territory; even if they had been carried there by the owner, with the intention of becoming a permanent resident. . . .

Thus the Court declared that every resolve of the Congress relating to free soil was a nullity. Up to this point, most people in the North and West had not become excited to any great degree over slavery within the Territories—the drumbeat of the abolitionists and the dire predictions of the planters notwithstanding. Now it was another matter.

Their immediate fear was that Federal courts would force slavery down their throats, despite their long traditions as free states. That decision gave added impetus to the abolitionist movement, and added fuel to the antislavery Republican Party. Three years later, the new party placed its first candidate in the White House, and the Union was no more.

The Presidential election of 1860 displayed the hopeless rifts within the American mind. Lincoln was the Republican nominee, pledged to the maintenance of free soil for the North, the West, and the Territories. Douglas, the moderate, accepted the Dred Scott decision, and received the nomination of the regular Democrats. Southerners, unsuccessful in placing a proslavery plank in the Democratic platform, nominated John C. Breckinridge of Kentucky. What was left of the Whig Party combined with the Know-Nothings to create a Constitutional Unionist Party, committed to maintenance of the Union and some moderation of the slavery question. Their nominee was John C. Bell of Tennessee. The North divided between Lincoln and Douglas, the South between Breckinridge and Bell. Lincoln, with only 40 per cent of the popular votes, nonetheless captured a decisive majority of votes in the electoral college.

The election of a Republican pledged to exclude slavery from the Territories, to a protective tariff, a Homestead Act, and a transcontinental railroad from the old Northwest to the Pacific was viewed as intolerable by the South.

The long struggle was nearing its climax. There was no ground left for compromise. On December 20, 1860, South Carolina passed the first Ordinance of Secession. Within three months, Mississippi, Florida, Alabama, Georgia,

Louisiana, and Texas had left the Union to form the Confederate States of America. The Union was split asunder.

The question that religious leaders had overlooked, that the Founders had bypassed, and that the peacemakers had postponed, had now come to full proportions. The "firebell in the night" was ringing, not in dreams, but in cold reality. Slavery had grown from "20 negars" in 1619 to destroy the Union in 1861.

4

Southern hopes for a bloodless secession, and Northern hopes for an amicable settlement and reunion, were doomed. Firebrands on both sides of the Potomac pushed the two sections closer to armed conflict. At last, on April 12, 1861, a shore battery of Confederate artillery fired upon the Union troops at Fort Sumter, in Charleston Bay, and the Civil War had begun.

It is not the purpose of this volume to chronicle that long and bloody conflict. Scholarly treatises abound on practically every phase of the war, and with the recent Centennial Celebration, the American people have been refreshed adequately upon the moving events and the drama of that dark time of peril.

Let it be noted here only that Federal troops and Federal arms overwhelmed a gallant but hopelessly outnumbered Confederacy. The men of the South established for all time their courage and devotion. They did not stop to count the costs, or to calculate the odds. The women of the South were no less brave, and their sacrifices for their husbands and sons in the field make a touching story of dauntless fidelity. Blessed with an abundance of military genius, with men well-attuned to the rigors of outdoor life and skilled in the arts of weaponry, the South at first won startling victories over mediocre Northern forces.

But military prowess and courage alone could not long resist the remorseless clanking of Northern factories, the relentless pressure of the Northern blockade, and the seemingly endless supply of Northern troops. The end had to come, as it did at Appomattox Courthouse, on April 9, 1865, when General Robert E. Lee, the outstanding soldier of the conflict, surrendered to General U. S. Grant.

The war was over. The North had won. The South had lost.

That war is not the province of this writing. The South, and her people, are. However, one event during the war bears special mention, as it bears most directly upon the shattering changes that lay in wait for the South of Reconstruction.

After open warfare had commenced, Lincoln came under increasing pressure to abolish slavery through the exercise of extraordinary war powers. Lincoln's political position was tenuous. The border states had not seceded, although many of their residents were sympathetic to the South. Successive victories of Southern forces were pushing them closer to a break with the Union. Lincoln feared that abolition might drive these states to a welcoming Confederacy, further weakening the North. Hence, the President replied that he was interested, not in the abolition of slavery, but in the preservation of the Union:

> If I could save the Union without freeing *any* slave, I would do it; and if I could save it by freeing *all* the slaves, I would do it; and if I could do it by freeing some and leaving others alone, I would also do that. . . . I intend no modification of my oft-expressed *personal* wish that all men, everywhere, could be free.

Lincoln's moderation on the subject pleased no one. Abolitionists were angered at what he had not done. Border citizens were apprehensive at what he might do. Then the President devised the master political stroke of his career.

After the first substantive Northern victory, at Antietam, in September of 1862, Lincoln signed the Emancipation Proclamation, which was to become effective on January 1, 1863.

Many erroneously believe that this act consummated the long struggle for freedom, and put an end to human bondage in America. The Proclamation is generally regarded as a high moral note struck during hours of dark national peril.

Yet, an honest viewer could with justification conclude it to be little more than wartime politics.

For those 3,063,393 slaves in the South—no longer a part of the Union—the document purported to bestow immediate and absolute freedom. Of course, that freedom could only be enforced by Federal arms, which thus far had met with notable lack of success. For the 441,702 slaves within the border states, still within the Union, and for slaves in other areas of the North, there was no freedom of any kind—conditional, qualified, or future. For the slaves in certain counties of Tennessee and Virginia which had already submitted to Federal rule, there was no freedom. And for the slaves in the nation's capital itself, there was continued bondage.

By the Emancipation Proclamation, Lincoln left untouched for nonseceding slaveholders their property rights in their fellow human beings, while, at the same time, undertaking to bestow freedom upon those slaves over whom the Union as yet had no control. Further, the provisions for the occupied portions of Tennessee and Virginia were designed to persuade other Southern areas to submit to the North, and thereby continue their property holdings.

The move was an immediate success, for world opinion rarely stops to read the fine print. Great Britain, which was pro-Southern in sympathy, ceased work on Confederate vessels of war. And at home the Federals added 50,000 Negro troops and labor conscripts to their forces in the field.

Perhaps Lincoln moved as far as he could without new danger to the Union. Perhaps the Emancipation Proclamation was publicly expedient and politically sound. Yet, it was hardly a great "Charter of Liberty."

The entire process underscores a point that should be clearly understood in American history—the Negro was rarely regarded by either side as a fellow human being. He was at first an atom in an agrarian society, of no more human concern to North or South than any other agricultural implement. He was next a fraction in a legislative apportionment formula, important only for the resulting number of Representatives his combined numbers would place in the House of Representatives. Then he became a condition attached to certain geographical units, which were determined to be either free or slave, with resultant effect upon the balance of power within the United States Senate. At the time of the Emancipation Proclamation, he became an alluring property right to states which acknowledged the Union, and a rod of punishment for states which disavowed it.

Hapless, ignorant, totally dependent, and desperately poor, his lot would not be any better for many years to come. Yet in the end the slave became the South's enslaver. It was his existence that ultimately committed her to an impossible conflict and a lost cause.

Yet, the institution of slavery was by no means universal to the South. In 1860, out of 1,516,000 white families in the South, there were only 385,000 slaveholders. Three-fourths of all white Southerners had no direct connection with slavery.

The "planter class" included those who owned 20 or more slaves. But 80 per cent of slave owners had fewer than this number, and 50 per cent had fewer than 5 slaves. The planter aristocracy was limited to about 10,000 families which worked gangs of 50 slaves or more. Fewer than 3,000 of these families owned as many as 100 slaves. Clearly, the majority of the 4 million slaves in the South belonged to the families of the planter class, not to the small farmers.

The planters ruled the South. They determined its politics and policies. They controlled education, the clergy, commerce, and the press. The poor white left his small farm untilled or his small shop untended to go off to war and do battle for the planter. He gave his life for an economic system to which he was hardly privy. He gave up his small holdings to protect and defend his neighbor's large holdings. The Southern wife gave her husband to protect the planter's slaves.

Who, then, was more the slave? The black man, born in bondage, who lived to be freed—or the white man, born free, who died that another might continue to enjoy his chattels?

It would be far from accurate to ascribe to the Confederate soldier the sole motive of preserving slavery. Manifestly, this was not the case. Once the lines had been drawn, Southern concepts of patriotism, liberty, and loyalty, along with protection of home and hearth, were ample and justifiable cause for taking up arms, and dying in battle if need be. Yet slavery, and all it entailed, was the central force that impelled North and South into conflict.

In the final analysis, the Confederate soldier died for another man's slave. An outstanding Southern observer, W. J. Cash, explained this paradox in his classic volume, *The Mind of the South*:

> The common white, as a matter of course, gave eager credence to and took pride in the legend of aristocracy which was so valuable to the defense of the land. He . . . felt his planter neighbor's . . . splendor as being in some fashion his also.

The victims of slavery were not all black.

* * *

At the end of the Civil War, a beaten and prostrate South lay at the mercy of a victorious North. Lincoln, who had counseled moderation, was dead. In his place stood Andrew Johnson, a man in whom few had confidence.

On May 20, 1865, six weeks after Appomattox, President Johnson revealed his plan for the "reconstruction" of the South. Briefly, the plan required that Southern states void their secession ordinances and ratify the Thirteenth Amendment abolishing slavery; that debts incurred by the Confederate Government be voided; that holders of public office subscribe to an oath of allegiance; and that new elections be held for state legislatures and for representation in Congress. Once again, the Negro, as a human being, was eliminated from consideration. There was nothing to prevent Southern legislatures from rapidly passing the "Black Codes," laws restricting severely the activities and conduct of Negroes. The terms Johnson offered were satisfactory to the South, and within six months every Confederate state had met them.

While the plan was generally accepted by the South, strong voices of protest arose in the North. Northerners and Republicans feared that the readmission of Southern states might restore the South's old dominance in Congress. Then, too, there was a heated outcry for retribution against the defeated states. The Johnson plan was scored as entirely too lenient by those who sought still harsher retaliation.

When the 37th Congress convened on December 4, 1865, the lines had hardened. Representatives of the Southern states presented themselves, expecting to be admitted to the chambers of Congress. Northern Members refused to admit them. Instead, they created a Joint Committee on Reconstruction, maintaining that the entire subject matter was Congressional rather than Executive in nature. In April of 1866, the Joint Committee, still without Southern members, reported the first Civil Rights Bill, and, in June, proposed the Fourteenth Amendment. Strangely enough, the Amendment failed of initial ratification because it was opposed by the North. The Kentucky, Ohio, Delaware, Maryland, and New Jersey legislatures all rejected the proposal.

Many Northerners had plans for a defeated South that

differed substantially from the views held by Lincoln and the plans proposed by Johnson. Their scheme was embodied in the Reconstruction Act, which Congress passed and Andrew Johnson promptly vetoed. The President rightly gauged its intent as punitive and detrimental to the restoration of the Union. Nonetheless, on March 2, 1867, responding to the leadership of Representative Thaddeus Stevens and Senator Charles Sumner, Congress overrode the veto, and the law was enacted.

A brief comparison with the Johnson plan shows the harsh judgment Northern Congressmen were determined to mete out to their Southern neighbors. The new act divided the South into five military districts, and established military government and martial law within each. New constitutional conventions were required in each Confederate state, with delegates to be chosen by universal adult male suffrage. Congress retained veto power over the constitutions so adopted. The state legislatures were required to ratify the Fourteenth Amendment, which would of necessity disqualify for office and disfranchise many former Confederates. When all this had been done, Congress magnanimously bestowed upon the compliant states the privilege of applying for readmission to the Union.

While it is profitless to speculate upon the legality of the Fourteenth Amendment—for long ago the nation recognized the necessity and worth of its central portions—it is nonetheless revealing to explore its legitimacy. As previously noted, ratifications by Northern states were insufficient for its adoption. The Southern states, not yet returned to the fold, were required to ratify because of

Northern refusal to ratify. The North saw the Negro franchise and Confededate disfranchisement as a secure means of diminishing Southern agricultural and regional interest, and keeping Southern states in a grossly inferior position.

All the while, the true interests of the Negro, in whose name so much had been perpetrated, were almost ignored and forgotten by Northern power.

During the years 1868 to 1870, the Southern states met the new conditions of the first Reconstruction Act. Southern legislatures were dominated by newly freed slaves, as were the Southern Congressional delegations. Many were, though through no fault of their own, completely illiterate, and the entire situation was ripe for corruption.

Obviously, the dark stain of Reconstruction is not due to any inherent vice on the part of the Negro, but rather to centuries of carefully enforced ignorance, the conniving of rapacious Northerners who followed the troops for public plunder, the disfranchisement of responsible whites, the total destruction of the economy, and the ruination of Southern lands.

It was naturally intolerable to a proud people, who had fought honorably on the field of arms, now to be suppressed by Radicals and strangers.

There developed in the South, as might have been expected, a total defiance to Radical rule. Bloodshed was common. Rioting, night-riding, and terror—on both sides—had more effect on the course of affairs than the governments of the states. The Ku Klux Klan and similar groups among whites, and Union League, among Negroes, contributed to the anarchy of the day.

Reconstruction was hard times.

Eliza Frances Andrews of Georgia, in her book, *The War-Time Journal of a Georgia Girl, 1864–1865,* described her homeland:

> About three miles from Sparta we struck burnt country. . . . The fields were trampled down and the road was lined with carcasses of hogs, horses, and cattle that the invader had wantonly shot down. . . . The stench in some places was unbearable. . . . The dwellings that were standing all showed signs of pillage, and on every plantation we saw the charred remains of the ginhouse. . . . Total homes laid in ashes. Hayricks and fodder stacks were demolished, corn cribs were empty, and every bale of cotton burnt. . . . There was not even a chicken left in the country to eat.

And William Colbert, a Georgia freedman, furnishes a touching picture of the crumbling of the old order:

> The Yankees come in, and they pull the fruit off the trees and et it. They et the hams and corn. They just stay round long enough to get plenty of something to eat. . . . The massa had three boys go to war, but there wasn't a one come home. All the children he had died. Massa, he lost all his money, and the house soon began dropping away to nothing. Us niggers one by one lef the old place, and last time I seed the home Plantation I was standing on a hill. I looked back on it for the last time, and it looked so lonely. There wa'n't but one person in sight, the massa. He was a-settin' in a wicker chair in the yard looking out over a small field of cotton and corn. There was four crosses in the graveyard in the side lawn where he was a-settin'. The fourth one was his wife. . . .

The white Southerner surely felt himself helpless, the pawn of a higher power in Federal uniform. His fields were burned, his livestock butchered, his voice silenced.

But there was another Southerner for whom Reconstruction was no easy lot. The slave was now free. What did freedom mean? A former slave explained: "I am now my own mistress, and need not work when I am sick. I can do my own thinking without having anyone to think for me—to tell me when to come, what to do, and sell me when they get ready." That was freedom. But, as Frederick Douglass, the best known ex-slave, said in his *Life and Times*, it was hardly enough.

And yet the government had left the freedman in a bad condition. It felt that it had done enough for him. It had made him free, and henceforth he must make his own way in the world. Yet he had none of the conditions of self-preservation or self-protection. . . . He had neither money, property, nor friends. He was free from the old plantation, but he had nothing but the dusty road under his feet. He was free from the old quarter that once gave him shelter, but a slave to the rains of summer and to the frosts of winter. He was . . . turned loose, naked, hungry, and destitute, to the open sky.

An account in the Montgomery *Advertiser* for August 18, 1865, chronicled a common response of many Negroes to the hardships that accompanied their new freedom:

Nine hundred Negroes assembled near Mobile. They resolved that they had discovered that the prejudices of color were by no means confined to the people of the South, but on the contrary, that it was stronger and more marked against them in the stranger from the North. . . . That Negroes no more than whites can live without work, or be comfortable

123

without homes; that their Northern deliverers from bondage had not undertaken to provide for their happy existence in their new state of freedom, and that their old masters had ceased to take any interest in them, or have a care for them; and . . . it was their deliberate conclusion that they should return to the homes which they had abandoned in a moment of excitement, and go to work again under their old masters.

The Federal Government was not wholly insensitive to this situation. It created the Freedmen's Bureau, designed to ease and speed transition from slavery to full citizenship. No one can quarrel with its aims, and its initial efforts proved quite beneficial to the former slaves. The Bureau issued 21 million rations during the period 1865–72, 15 million going to Negroes and the rest to destitute whites. During its six years of existence, the Bureau put over five million dollars into public schools for Negroes, employing 3,300 teachers for 146,581 pupils.

But, like other Radical programs of that time, it soon became enmeshed in graft and corruption of the most outrageous sort. Unscrupulous Northern whites moved in, seeing the opportunity to exploit Negroes for their own selfish ends. They established among them militaristic Union Leagues, collecting dues which lined their pockets.

Republicans, playing upon the deep religious nature of Negroes, sought their political support by reminding them that the Bible divided men into two classes—"Publicans and Sinners."

J. S. Fullerton, of the Louisiana Freedmen's Bureau, commented upon its operation in that state:

> On the part of some agents there has been a want of tact, conciliation and sound judgment. Their prejudices so blinded

them that they could not properly approach the people with whom they had to deal, and it appears as though they went to the South to foster disunion, rather than to cure and heal. In many cases they have produced inveterate enmity between whites and blacks, instead of bringing about the good understanding and respect that their mutual interests require.

In spite of the excesses of some of its personnel, the Bureau did accomplish some good. It supplied to many the bare necessities of life which they otherwise would have lacked. It provided a smattering of schooling to some. It was the only social agency operating in the entire South. But the task was too great. Most of the Bureau's activities came to an end in 1869, though its educational effort lasted until 1872.

The Freedmen's Bureau was another opportunity lost. It was an effort to lift the Negro, prostrate from long years of slavery, up from the dust and into a full life. It sought to educate him, clothe him, instruct him in basic agricultural and mechanical arts, and make him self-sufficient. It sought to help him help himself. It was a Poverty Program one hundred years ahead of its time. Had it succeeded, today's and tomorrow's generations might have been spared their heavy burdens. But it failed, and its failure is clear warning to us today. Inadequate administrators, inadequate funds, and inadequate patience with the vexing problems of poverty produce inadequate results. Today's failure will surely add to tomorrow's responsibility.

It soon became apparent that Washington's plan for Reconstruction would fail, and for several years Northerners pressed for some provision to secure the rights of new citizens. Finally, on March 1, 1875, they succeeded in enacting the Civil Rights Act of 1875. It provided:

> That all persons within the jurisdiction of the United States shall be entitled to the full and equal enjoyment of the accommodations, advantages, facilities, and privileges of inns, public conveyances on land or water, theatres and other places of public amusement; subject only to the conditions and limitations established by law, and applicable alike to citizens of every race and color, regardless of any previous condition of servitude.

Agitation for the Civil Rights Bill probably did more than Republican misrule in placing Alabama in the Democratic column in the Presidential election of 1872. Many small farmers in northern Alabama had consistently voted Republican. Yet the specter of Negro equality so alarmed them that they went over in a body to the Democratic ticket. Ninety-two years later, history would reverse itself.

The Act had little practical effect. It served often as a weapon of demagoguery in the hands of Democrats. Frequently, just before elections, Northern Democrats would hire Negroes to board in white hotels, eat in white restaurants, and othewise "assert" their equality. These tactics had telling effects upon Northern Republicans, who favored equality in the South, but felt that their own states were "different."

By 1874, only four Southern states—Florida, Mississippi, South Carolina, and Louisiana—remained under military rule.

Two years later, the outcome of the Hayes-Tilden contest merely affirmed what was already the case—that Radicals could not impose their will upon the South in face of Southern resistance. Accordingly, the removal of the troops after the Bargain was not of critical importance. It marked, however, the end of Radical efforts to rule the South. It marked, also, an abandonment of the Negro to the predominant element of Southern whites who were determined that his new citizenship should be second-class.

There is a great lesson to be learned, on both sides, from the toils and failures of Reconstruction.

The North undertook to impose its will by political oppression and military force. It disfranchised the responsible Southern whites. It deprived them of their resources by wiping out the Confederate debt. It brought about radical new departures at the bayonet's point. It suffered hordes of profit seekers and plunderers to flood into the South, while withholding any protection from their depredations.

The South, defeated and helpless, utterly rejected any notion of reasoned adjustment to new conditions. Rather, it fed upon its own bitterness. It failed to view the newly freed Negro as a citizen in its midst, requiring massive and charitable help, but saw him only as the tool of its hated oppressors.

Reconstruction was a failure. From this period, the white Southerner developed phobias that are with him today. The Negro Southerner found his new freedom to be little more than a slightly revised serfdom. Relationships between the two races were hardened in a mold that only today is beginning to crack.

What might have been? The war was over, the fighting done. The old order of master and slave was broken. Loss to planters through emancipation was not an insurmountable blow to the general economy. Here was an opportunity, through prudence, firmness, patience, and common sense, to create a new order of free men. Here was a chance to extend the great principles of the Declaration of Independence to that one-third of the South who had lived for centuries in the outer darkness. Here was a chance for Northerners to turn their preachments into reality for four million downtrodden Americans, newly become citizens.

But Northern interest, power, and revenge combined with Southern defiance, terror, and scorn to foreclose that hope. Truthfully, there was little hope for successful reunion. The North never once considered whether it had a duty to people of the South—in rebuilding a shattered economy, and developing responsible Southern leadership. There was no Marshall Plan, no Economic Recovery Program, no Alliance for Progress. Instead, Northern efforts were more punitive than restorative.

The South barely considered any course other than violent and unremitting opposition to a course of Northern conduct it deemed unjust and oppressive. There was no communication, no understanding, no sympathy between victor and vanquished—only the rod of the conqueror and the stripes of the captive.

Between these two forces, the Southern freedman was little more than what he had been before, the pawn of vastly superior warring interests which took little note of him as a citizen or as a human soul.

❖　　❖　　❖

Slavery was dead. Segregation in public places had been outlawed by the Civil Rights Act of 1875. The Negro was a citizen, with full franchise rights. The Fourteenth Amendment, now ratified by Southern states, afforded him the equal protection of the laws. That was what the lawbooks said.

But the facts did not match the lofty preambles and ringing legal phrases. In fact, the South of 1880 was not too different from the South of 1860. The Negro was freed, to become a sharecropper on land he could never hope to own without the intervention of some unusual circumstance. He was a free man, except for his soul, which he owed to the company store. He could vote, and sometimes, if he voted right, the election managers would count his ballot. He could go to the theater, if he had the money and the nerve—that is, until 1883, when the Supreme Court declared the Civil Rights Act of 1875 unconstitutional. Above all, he was desperately poor—and this condition changed little during the remainder of the nineteenth century.

The South, black and white, endured long years of hardship after the war. Times were easy for no one. Cotton was the sole crop, and upon the difference of a penny or two in price depended the fortune of millions of Southerners. Local capital was practically nonexistent, and what industry there had been was a casualty of the war.

Because cotton was a Southern product, and because Southern labor was cheap, it was natural that textile mills should move South. Mill wages included the right to live in some sort of house owned by the company, either free or for a dollar or so a week. Money payments ranged from 20 cents a day for bobbin boys, through 40 to 60 cents a day for spinners, to a dollar a day for weavers, the aristocrats of the mill. This was somewhat more than half the

129

wage rate paid in the mills of New England. At best, counting housing and other benefits, the Southern wage was two-thirds that of the North. The average work week in the Southern mills was 68 to 72 hours, compared to 56 to 58 hours in New England.

Edgar G. Murphy wrote of an Alabama mill in 1904:

> I have seen children called to work before sunup and dismissed from work only after sunset, laboring from dark to dark—13 to 14 hours per day. I have seen children eight and nine years of age leaving the factory as late as 9:30 and finding their way with their own little lanterns through the unlighted streets of the mill village to their squalid homes.

The Southern factory was almost invariably organized on the model of the familiar plantation of the cotton fields. W. J. Cash described the new mill economy in his book, *The Mind of the South*:

> . . . [The mill owners] had . . . long been accustomed to looking upon themselves as the saviors of the South and the conferrers of benefactions upon both their workmen and the public at large . . . .
>
> The body of the Southern people . . . were . . . innocent of the implications inherent in modern industrialism—of the notion that when men are brought together in large numbers and made absolutely dependent on capital for the right to earn their daily bread, they can no longer be dealt with by the standards of property . . . which prevail in an agricultural or handiwork community . . . .
>
> As they saw it . . . the mills were their owners' to do with wholly as they pleased, without regard to anything but their own will, just as a thirty-acre farm was the farmer's or a house was the householder's. The master of the mill had the right to set wages and hours at whatever figure he chose.

And if the workman didn't like them—this was a free country, and it was his right to reject them or to quit. And if that in practice meant his right to starvation for himself and his wife and children? Let him take what he could get, save his money, and he wouldn't have to put up with it long. A lot of rich men had started poor, hadn't they?

John Calhoun's followers could no longer point the finger of accusation at the wage slaves of the North. Now the South had her share, at two-thirds of Northern wages.

The increase of industrial employment and the continued plight of small farmers gave rise to a new movement in the late nineteenth century, based upon a coalition of small farmers and laborers. The People's Party, or Populists, sought adherents from both races. Theretofore, all whites had been Democrats, and the only Republicans had been Negroes and a few carpetbaggers. But the Populists appealed to all the poor, black and white alike. In 1892, the People's Party captured over a million votes in the Presidential election. Their platform demanded decent wages, an increase in the money supply, a graduated income tax, a postal savings system, the secret ballot, protection of labor, and control of monopolies. It was a challenging platform, and has long since been incorporated into the laws of the nation. Populism in the South was primarily agrarian. The party had something to offer in the nature of direct, tangible, immediate economic benefit to all farmers of the South.

In Georgia, Populists sent Thomas E. Watson to Congress. Watson's election, and the support he was gathering over the state, constituted a substantial challenge to the Democratic Party. A workable combination of Negroes and poor whites could produce substantial majorities throughout the South. A combination of farmers and laborers would mean similar majorities throughout the nation.

The Democrats, threatened by the new movement, were not long in responding to demands for better working conditions and curtailment of the abuses of great wealth. They had a simple answer—"Negro domination." They played it well, conjuring up the old specters of rape and corruption, and drove the Populists apart. Tom Watson was defeated, and turned upon his former Negro constituents, who were soon remanded to their old place of impotence within the Republican Party.

To properly focus the dangers posed by the Populist movement, the Democrats pushed through Southern state legislatures a series of laws providing for strict separation of the races, known collectively as Jim Crow. Years earlier, following emancipation, Southern legislatures had passed similar laws, called Black Codes. These were essentially the old slave regulations in new form. Carpetbag legislatures had promptly repealed most of them. Now, thirty-five years later, the Southern states again turned their attention to legalizing what had for the most part been *de facto* all the while.

Before 1900, there were few segregation statutes. But then they came in rapid succession. By 1915, South Carolina had gone so far as to prohibit textile factory workers of different races from using the same rooms, entrances, pay windows, exits, doors, lavatories, toilets, drinking water buckets, pails, cups, dippers or glasses—at any time.

State institutions for the care of dependent or incapacitated persons were subject to more legislation than private institutions. Thirteen states required the separation of

132

patients by race in mental hospitals, and ten in penal institutions. Two states required Negro nurses for Negro patients. North Carolina and Florida required that textbooks used by public-school children of one race be kept separate from those used by the other. Florida law specified that separation be maintained even while the books were in storage. South Carolina required a *third* set of books for mulattoes.

Streetcar segregation was not required by law until after the turn of the century. It is ironic that the first city to adopt a streetcar ordinance was Montgomery, Alabama, in the year 1906. There is where it began, and there is where it began to crumble with the bus boycott fifty years later.

It has been noted that Negro suffrage existed in theory but not in fact. The anti-Populist reaction put a stop to this. An ingenious combination of poll taxes, grandfather clauses, and white primaries soon disfranchised the Negro in theory as well. Primary laws were adopted in South Carolina in 1896, in Arkansas in 1897, in Georgia in 1898, in Florida and Tennessee in 1901, in Alabama and Mississippi in 1902, in Kentucky and Texas in 1903, in Louisiana in 1906, in Oklahoma in 1907, in Virginia in 1913, and in North Carolina in 1915. The effect of these laws is clearly apparent from registration figures. For example, in 1896 there were 130,334 registered Negro voters in Louisiana. By 1904 there were only 1,342.

The changeover from a strict cotton economy to a substantial measure of new industry was another opportunity for the South—white and black. Populism, had it taken hold, could have brought to the poor farmer and the laborer of both races a vastly enhanced economic stature.

The two could have joined hands in a powerful combination, and presented a common front to the absentee landowner, the commissary, and the mill operator. Sharecropper and mill worker could have stood on equal ground with the banks, railroads, textile and land interests. Decent textile wages could have raised the general level of well-being for millions of Southerners, increased their buying power, enhanced the value of real property, raised tax revenues, provided decent public services, and built a stronger, happier, fairer South.

But the opportunity was lost. The old ways, not the new, prevailed. The poor white heeded the ancient cry of "nigger," and turned upon his own interest. Rejecting the rationality of Populism, he rushed like the lemming into the sea to be submerged anew by the old interests and the old powers. In so doing, he condemned his family, his children, and in a measure his children's children, to relive his own unhappy lot.

And there, for both races, the matter rested for many years.

❋   ❋   ❋

The twentieth century has witnessed the growth of the United States from a nation of 76 million people to one whose population is reaching toward 200 million; from an insular, self-centered nation to a world power whose commitments and responsibilities reach into every corner of the globe; from an economy with a gross national product of 17 billion dollars to one producing almost 700 billion dollars' worth of goods and services a year. We have come a long way indeed in sixty-odd years.

Yet in one area of our national life—in the matter of race—we have advanced scarcely more than a step since the turn of the century, and what progress has been made has taken place primarily within the last decade.

This generation has seen its own lost opportunities. One was the New Deal.

In 1933, President Franklin D. Roosevelt held the nation in the palm of his hand. The famous "One Hundred Days" following his first inauguration are unparalleled in our history. Congress, anxious to do anything that would raise the smothering pall of the Depression, readily responded to every suggestion the President placed before it. Some bills were passed without reference to any committee, and without hearings, report, rule, or debate. On occasion, the Congress enacted measures evidenced solely by the typewritten copy sent over from the White House.

It was, indeed, a new deal. The Federal Government assumed vast economic powers never before exercised. Sweeping controls were mounted over many phases of the nation's economy. New revenues were sought. New deficits were incurred. New money was placed in circulation. New conditions were imposed upon labor and management, farmer and businessman, rich and poor. Vast new public works projects rose from the dust of a broken economy. The mills began to hum, the factories began to smoke. The nation was finally on the move again.

Roosevelt knew the South as a frequent visitor and a concerned friend. His famous address on the South is widely quoted today:

> It is my conviction that the South presents right now the nation's number one economic problem—the nation's problem, not merely the South's. For we have an economic unbalance in the nation as a whole, due to this very condition of the South. It is an unbalance that can and must be

135

righted, for the sake of the South and the nation. Without going into the long history of how this situation came to be —the long and ironic history of the despoiling of this truly American section of the country's population—suffice it for the immediate purpose to get a clear perspective of the task presented to us.

That task embraces the wasted or neglected resources of land and water, the abuses suffered by the soil, the need for cheap fertilizer and cheap power; the problems presented by the population itself, the problems presented by the South's capital resources and the absentee ownership of those resources, and problems growing out of the new industrial era and, again, of absentee ownership of new industries. There is the problem of labor and employment in the South and the related problem of protecting women and children in this field. There is the problem of farm ownership of which farm tenancy is a part, and of farm income. There are questions of taxation, of education, of housing, and of health.

The National Emergency Committee of New Deal days had a specific responsibility concerning the problems of the South. It summed up the long-term economic effects of agrarianism, slavery, Reconstruction, one-crop eccnomy, and the whole pace of Southern history:

So much of the profit from Southern industries goes to outside financiers in the form of dividends and interest, that state income taxes would produce a meager yield in comparison with similar levies elsewhere. State taxation does not reach dividends which flow to corporation stockholders and management in other states; and as a result these people do not pay their share of the cost of Southern schools and other institutions. . . .

For mining its mineral wealth and shipping it away in a raw or semifinished form, the South frequently receives nothing but the low wages of unskilled and semi-skilled labor. The wages for manufacturing this natural wealth into finished products often do not go to Southerners, but to workers in other areas; and the profits likewise usually go to financial institutions in other regions. When a Southerner buys the finished product, on the other hand, the price he pays includes all the wasteful cross-hauling involved in the present system. . . .

The South, in fact, has been caught in a vise that has kept it from moving along with the mainstream of American economic life. . . . Penalized for being rural, and handicapped in its efforts to industrialize, the economic life of the South has been squeezed to the point where the purchasing power of Southern people does not provide an adequate market for its own industries, nor an attractive market for those of the rest of the country.

The Depression struck the South with full force. A poor section, its poverty was keener than that of others. Having fewer resources to fall back on, it exhausted them the sooner.

It was a time that required vast changes. New programs had to be fashioned. It was a matter of strict and compelling necessity, for times of crisis require radical changes. And new programs did come trooping from Washington. The whole panorama of New Deal programs was applied to Southern problems. The South, so long hesitant to change, was willing to give Roosevelt and the New Deal a try.

Yet there was one area that remained beyond the innovations that swirled over the South. There was no change in Jim Crow. There was no New Deal for the Negro. Nor was there any discernible modification of

Southern attitudes. In the absence of a nationwide consensus for change—a consensus that developed only after thirty years more—the New Deal maintained a policy of deference to old attitudes. Again, the problem of the Negro was postponed to another day.

World War II brought many long-term changes to the South. Many thousands of young men, white and black, were uprooted and taken out of the South. Many of those who left never returned, and those who did, returned with new attitudes and new aspirations. For the first time in the nation's history, the postwar period witnessed widespread activity among Negroes directed to their own betterment, not only within the framework of old conditions, but outside them, and directed at changes in the old relationships. The period also saw the emergence of new and more militant Negro leaders speaking for those who had long been silent.

Yet little of this was reflected in the White House or in the Congress, the two branches of government supposedly most responsive to changing national needs. It was the Supreme Court, farthest removed from daily events and historically least sensitive to them, which finally, in 1954, ruled squarely against school segregation.

❋   ❋   ❋

At this point the honest observer and the realistic Southerner will be wise to consider the years of his past. For the burden of Southern history is lost opportunity.

Consider, for a moment, what might have happened at the very beginning, in 1619. The twenty "negars" of John Rolfe's diary arrived at Jamestown during the same season as the first legislative assembly in the New World.

Had these twenty come as free laborers, rather than mere chattels, the entire course of American history would have been drastically altered. Had the clergy of the colonies displayed the same zeal in the name of Christianity that Garrison was later to display in the name of abolition, public sentiment might have been mobilized against slavery at Philadelphia in 1787. Had the Founders written into their document their personal convictions, which were substantially opposed to slavery, the matter might then and there have been settled for all time.

Perhaps it is true that the series of compromises, beginning with Missouri in 1820, were dictated by circumstances already hard frozen, and served, at least, to preserve the Union for another forty years. But it is not at all beyond the realm of possibility that some more farsighted approach could have been found by both sides, North and South, whereby slavery would have been abolished, with some assistance to planters in transition from slave to free labor. And the war itself—had Northern efforts embodied compassion and generosity, and had Southern response accepted inevitable change—but another course was chosen. Here were two lost opportunities: first, Federal efforts to upgrade the lot and life of the freedman were too little, and abandoned too soon; second, Southern resistance to equality for all citizens frustrated whatever well-intentioned efforts were made. Reconstruction failed, and Southern resistance won—locking into place the lot of millions of the South's people for almost a century more.

The rise of Populism, espousing many programs which we deem essential to the welfare of the nation today, offered another opportunity to bind together Southerners of both races, in the common search for common betterment. But this, too, failed, when the two races were driven apart by the dominant party of the day. Populism's most eloquent Southern spokesman, Tom Watson, joined in the dispersion, heaping acrimony upon his Negro followers, raising the specter of "Negro domination," and spreading his wrath to include, along with his ancient economic enemies, new foes among the non-white, non-Southern, non-Protestant, and non-Gentile.

The New Deal, coming at a time of upheaval, could have bettered old social patterns, as it did old economic patterns. Recent history has continued the old pattern of the failure of the established order in the South either to maintain itself or to make realistic adjustments to change.

In 1954, the Supreme Court ruled. There was the chance to say, "We have been wrong. We shall henceforth be right." Instead, there followed massive resistance, interposition, and all the old maneuvers that had failed even so long ago as the time of John C. Calhoun. Then came Little Rock, New Orleans, Oxford—and Birmingham. Then the Civil Rights Act of 1964.

And even then the series of failures did not end. A few months later, defiance and disfranchisement brought about a new Voting Rights Act of 1965.

Throughout its long struggles, the Southern order has lost.

The Supreme Court decision of 1954 and all that followed in its wake have brought us now to a point of unrest and bitterness which no one desires, and all decry. Negroes are impatient with the pace of change. Whites are apprehensive. Incidents mount, tempers flare, threats abound, and violence flickers on the horizon.

In such a state, it is possible that the South can lose again. We can ignore history, and thereby relive it.

The characters and events of the past return to haunt the scenes of our lost opportunities. Calhoun cries "Never!" Garrison cries "Now!" Webster offers a middle course, and goes down in defeat. The old doctrine of Nullification becomes now interposition. The Ku Klux Klan of 1865 rides again. The Loyalty League of Reconstruction is now the Deacons for Defense. Federal Troops in blue kepis become Federal marshals in white helmets. Alabama farmers, who switched from Republicans to Democrats over the Civil Rights Act of 1875, have returned to the fold, impelled by the same fears which drove them forth. Southern Republicans drive apart the natural elements of the Democratic Party, as Southern Democrats once drove apart the natural allies of the Populist movement. Universal suffrage of Reconstruction becomes the literacy test ban of 1965. The Poverty Program takes up where the Freedmen's Bureau left off.

* * *

The North has never had the wit and the South has never had the will to solve the race problem. Vindictiveness from one quarter can combine with intransigence from the other, as they did one hundred years ago, and perpetuate themselves to the sorrow of the nation. But it need not be. We are *not* hopelessly condemned to relive history. Rather, if we have the wit and the will, we can add a new and brighter chapter to Southern history.

PART THREE

5

See those grey gulls balance against the sky?
As like as like, aren't they? It's better so.
I saw some fishermen snare one and tie
Red flannel to its leg, then let it go;
I watched it rise again, briefly to soar
Until its wheeling mates, catching the brave
Glint of the pennon, screamed their rage and tore
Its life away above a sobbing wave.

Never will I forgive them for that day
They sent a tortured sea gull up to die;
Yet in our town the most of us are grey
And don't like unasked colors in our sky
And, God be witness, there are few we spare
Whenever He ties scarlet here and there.
                         —Hodding Carter, "Palette"

The author of the brief poem quoted above has long been a clear and honest voice of reason within the South. He has viewed his native section with concern, compassion, and realism, and has understood well that the Southerner is somewhat a man apart, dwelling in a land apart. Few have captured better than Carter the brittleness of

145

Southern pride, and the deep attachment of the Southerner to Southern ways:

> The sense of intimate identification with a region fortifies
> the will to make it more nearly perfect and secure; and as
> the part is strengthened so is the whole. It is only when
> loyalty makes the regional patriot blind to imperfection and
> resentful of inspection that it becomes a deteriorative force;
> the obligation to examine, to protest and to propose change
> must accompany affection, else devotion can destroy. Too
> many Southerners fail to perceive this corollary; defiant and
> resentful of the alien critic, they are even more enraged at
> the native censor, stigmatizing him as a nest-fouler and
> suggesting that he should go elsewhere if he is not satisfied
> with what he finds.

Hostility to outside criticism, and its corollary, outrage
at criticism from within, have long been a part of the
Southern character. H. L. Mencken observed it in 1917,
in connection with an ordinance forbidding any trouser
presser in a small Georgia town from pressing for both
whites and Negroes. The town, like most small Southern
towns, was one in which practically all the white inhabitants had "their food prepared by colored hands, their
babies cared for by colored hands, and the clothes which
they wear right next to their skins washed in houses where
Negroes live, houses in which the said clothes remain for
as long as a week at a time." And Mencken commented:
"But if you marvel at the absurdity keep it dark. A casual
word, and the united press of the South will be upon your
trail, denouncing you bitterly as a scoundrelly damn
Yankee, a Bolshevik Jew."

One of my colleagues in the Congress, a man of education and compassion, told me a story that makes the same point:

"You know what's wrong with us?" he began. "The other night my wife and I were in our living room, and I said to her, 'These drapes don't hang right, and something is wrong with the whole color scheme.' She agreed, and we decided to have the whole thing done over. Then, a few days later, a friend of ours came over for supper. Before the evening was over, he said to us, 'Those drapes don't go with your wallpaper.' It made us both mad as hell. Now," he said, "that's what's wrong with the South."

Too often we resolve to make needful changes. Then the critics come, and we stiffen our necks. We become so incensed over the *fact* of criticism that we refuse to examine the *substance* of criticism. And woe be unto that Southerner who dares question for himself what others have reaffirmed throughout the years.

All Southerners have an indefinable pride in the South. It is, indeed, "a land apart." It is different from the rest of the country. Southerners are fond of each other. We like the way we talk; we like the courtesies that usually abound in Southern society. We like the Southern attitude about many things—a native wit, a personal generosity, a certain earthiness born from a closer association with the soil. We like the easy, friendly relationships that exist between one Southerner and another. We like the "country boy" that is present, in varying degree, in all Southerners. In short, we like the South. And there are not many Southerners, even the most severe critics of their region, who would choose to cast their lot elsewhere.

But to view the South realistically does not diminish the

147

affection that Southerners hold for their land. To advocate needful changes and new approaches is not to deny that affection. The Southerner who is devoted to his section should be the one most anxious to see it change for the better. The outstanding exemplar of such a Southerner is Thomas Jefferson.

No other public figure rivals Jefferson in the extent of his influence upon Southern thought. His name is constantly invoked in support of States' rights, interposition, Nullification, strict construction, and *laissez-faire*. But many who deem him their patron saint would be keenly disappointed by a proper appraisal of his mind, the development of his views, and his reaction to the necessities of domestic and foreign affairs.

For Jefferson's great quality, along with his unparalleled intellect, was the ability to adjust his opinions to the mandate of necessity. And it is this flexibility, this realism, this capacity for growth that is at once his greatest legacy and, curiously, the one facet of his mind that self-styled "Jeffersonians" of today studiously ignore.

For example, one of his first acts as President was to double the territory of the United States through the Louisiana Purchase. Eight hundred thousand square miles, from New Orleans to Canada and the Rocky Mountains, were acquired from Napoleon for 15 million dollars. That acquisition involved the new President in a Constitutional conflict, for nothing in the Constitution authorized the Chief Executive to purchase land. Jefferson had earlier rejected the concept of "implied powers," and felt that the action was beyond Federal authority. Yet, the prospect of losing Louisiana was unthinkable. So he concluded the Purchase, and *then* asked Congress for an amendment to the Constitution authorizing what he had already done. It was inconsistent with every interpretation he had made of the General Government. But it was imperative, and Jefferson did what had to be done.

Jefferson was a true radical. He accepted nothing as true that was not demonstrably true. As often as he committed his opinions to paper, almost as frequently did necessity require their alteration. The Louisiana Purchase is but one example. Another is found in his once almost violent scorn for cities and the urban masses. During one long period of hostility with the British, in order to prevent the impressment of American seamen, Congress, at Jefferson's request, passed the Embargo Act, halting all shipping from American ports. The commercial interests of New England were desperately jeopardized by the law, and Jefferson found it almost impossible to administer and enforce. This experience brought about a change in his outlook on the proper function of manufactures in the United States. He had formerly disdained commercial endeavors and looked entirely to the land as a source of wealth and prosperity, but now he was forced to consider how the people can supply themselves with the necessities —and luxuries—of life. In an address to the Society of Tammany in 1808, he revealed the direction of his new thoughts:

> There can be no question, in a mind truly American, whether it is best to send our citizens and property into certain captivity, and then wage war for their recovery, or to keep them at home, and to turn seriously to that policy which plants the manufacturer and the husbandman side by side, and establishes at the door of everyone that exchange of mutual labors and comforts, which we have hith-

erto sought in distant regions, and under perpetual risk of broils with them.

Such changes are totally consistent with Jefferson's own view of change. In his Second Inaugural Address, he chastised those who resist adjustment:

> These persons inculcate a sanctimonious reverence for the customs of their ancestors; that whatsoever they did, must be done through all time; that reason is a false guide, and to advance under its counsel, in their physical, moral, or political condition is perilous innovation; that their duty is to remain as their Creator made them, ignorance being safety, and knowledge full of danger; in short, my friends, among them is seen the action and counteraction of good sense and bigotry; they, too, have their anti-philosophers who find an interest in keeping things in their present state, who dread reformation, and exert all their faculties to maintain the ascendency of habit over the duty of improving our reason, and obeying its mandates.

And one of his most noted passages displays similar sentiment:

> Some men look at constitutions with sanctimonious reverence, and deem them like the ark of the covenant, too sacred to be touched. They ascribe to the preceding age a wisdom more than human, and suppose what they did to be beyond amendment. I know that age well. . . . It was very like the present, and forty years of experience in government is worth a century in book reading. . . . I am certainly not an advocate for frequent and untried changes in laws and institutions. . . . But I know also, that laws and institutions must go hand in hand with the progress of the human mind. As that becomes more developed, more enlightened, as new discoveries are made, new truths discovered, and manners and opinions change with the change of circumstances,

institutions must advance also, and keep pace with the times. We might as well require a man to wear still the coat that fitted him when a boy, as civilized society to remain ever under the regimen of their barbarous ancestors.

In 1807, when the Constitutional grace period for importation of slaves was expiring, he said of slavery:

Whatever may have been the circumstances which influenced our forefathers to permit the introduction of personal bondage into any part of these States, and to participate in the wrongs committed on an unoffending quarter of the globe, we may rejoice that such circumstances, and such a sense of them exist no longer. It is honorable to the nation at large that their legislature availed themselves of the first practicable moment for arresting the progress of this great moral and political error; and I sincerely pray with you, my friends, that all the members of the human family may, in the time prescribed by the Father of us all, find themselves securely established in the enjoyment of life, liberty, and happiness.

Jefferson, though a Southerner of Southerners, readily confessed the evil of slavery, and became the first prominent Southerner to advocate equal rights and citizenship for Negroes. Though he was an aristocrat, he wrote in 1776, "No wonder the oppressed should rebel, & they will continue to rebel & raise disturbance until their civil rights are fully restored to them & all partial distinctions, exclusions & incapacitations are removed." He was an agrarian, yet he came to see the absolute necessity for commercial and industrial expansion within the United States, and the inevitable rise of great centers of population. A man of personal wealth, his heart belonged to the poor and struggling masses. A principal architect of the Revolution and the Constitution, he was the first to acknowledge the folly of placing a cut-off date upon the advance of human wisdom and experience. For Thomas Jefferson, there were no "good old days," nor any immutable structure for government. "The creator has made the earth for the living, not the dead. . . . A generation may bind itself as long as its majority continues in life; when that has disappeared, another majority is in place, holds all the rights and powers their predecessors held, and may change their laws and institutions to suit themselves. Nothing is unchangeable but the inherent and unalienable rights of man."

Somehow, over the turmoil of the decades, Jefferson—whose very soul was life and free spirit and innovation and advancement and diffusion of the bounties of a fertile land—has been perverted into a symbol of harsh and immutable precepts. This does violence to a massive intellect, and a great spirit. Those advocates of the past, who would return to the good old "Jeffersonian" period, would do well to rid themselves of their delusions about what he said, and what he wrote, and what he was. "Nothing," as he said himself, "is unchangeable but the inherent and unalienable rights of man."

❖   ❖   ❖

All of us harbor a dream for the South. With some, it is an idealized version of the old planter days, with every man sitting beneath the shade of his own magnolia tree. With others it is a New South, perhaps as described by Henry Grady as long ago as 1887:

> I see a South, a home of 50 million people who rise up every day to call her blessed; her cities, vast hives of industry and thrift; her countrysides the treasures from which

their resources are drawn; her streams vocal with whirring spindles; her valleys tranquil in the white and gold of the harvest; her mountains showering down the music of bells, as her slow moving flocks and herds go forth from their folds; her rulers honest and her people loving, and her homes happy and their hearthstones bright, and their waters still, and their pastures green, and her conscience clear; her wealth diffused and poor houses empty, her churches earnest and all creeds lost in the gospel . . . her two races walking together in peace and contentment; sunshine everywhere and all the time.

Whatever his dream, the realistic Southerner knows that we must begin with the South of today, with its strength and weakness, its virtues and faults, its good and its bad. I am not unmindful of harsh resistance to native criticism, nor am I insensate to the pitfalls faced by any public man who sets his thoughts to paper. Thus, hoping for the best and expecting the worst, I come to the final portion of this brief work.

*   *   *

History moves, and it is within the power of men, insofar as it is consistent with the will of Providence, to chart its course. As the oarsman guides his vessel by looking over the stern at some fixed object on shore, so we can offer some direction to the course of events by observing where we have been.

But now we must ask where we are, and where we are going.

For if there is any lesson in the events we have examined, it is that for more than a century the South, through adherence to a lost cause, has lost. Cleaving to the institution of human slavery, the South's position was finally overrun by the admission of new, free states. Thinking continued union intolerable to its interests, the South seceded—and lost the war that followed. Mounting relentless resistance to the social and economic betterment of Southern Negroes during and after Reconstruction, the South welded a framework that has produced and reproduced vast numbers of Southerners who contribute little or nothing to their communities, but rather constitute a heavy drag upon already meager public resources.

In later years, all the wiles and wisdom of Southern lawyers, backed by all the tax moneys of Southern states, could not, in the end, evade or forestall the Supreme Court decision of 1954. And the excesses of cattle prods, fire hoses, church bombings, and voting prohibitions generated national legislation that could not be thwarted by all the parliamentary skill of Southerners, and all their accumulated seniority in the Congress.

It is time now for the South to stop losing, and to start winning.

*　　*　　*

Southerners should first consider the costs of losing, and the gains that will come from winning.

In recent years the nation has reached a firm accord on the principle that no one should be denied equal opportunity by the mere accident of birth. As that worthy proposition applies to race, it must also apply to region. Specifically, it must apply to the South. The child born south of the Mason-Dixon Line must have a future equally as bright as that awaiting the child of the East, or North, or West. That Southern children do not enjoy that equality of opportunity should be a challenge for every Southerner.

Why, for instance, should Southerners be satisfied that Southern children are shortchanged in their education? A public-school child in New York receives the benefit of $705 per year spent on his education. A Mississippi child gets only $241. Is a New York child three times as valuable to the country as a Mississippi child? Certainly not. Yet the accident of birth in Mississippi imposes severe disadvantages upon public-school students. Nor does the South as a whole do much better than Mississippi. The national average expenditure per student is $455 per year. Not one Southern state meets that standard. The combined average for the South is $320 per pupil. Are children over the nation worth one-third more than Southern children? Surely not.

Should a Southern child have lesser economic expectations than his counterpart elsewhere in the nation? Per capita annual income in the South is substantially lower than the national average of $2,366, and not one Southern state meets that average. Annual income per capita ranges from $1,285 in Mississippi to $2,044 in Florida. Only Texas, Virginia, and Florida—not Deep South states—rank higher than fortieth out of the fifty states.

Should Southerners expect to be poor? The South has just under 15 million families—about one-third of all the families in the country. But of all the families in the nation with less than $2,000 annual income, fully one-half are Southern. Half the Negro families in the South fall in this unhappy category.

But the cost of living, it is sometimes said, is lower in the South than in the North, and therefore we need not be so concerned. Here is an old myth. It is an excuse, as well as an illusion.

The cost of living is lower in the South, if the Southerner is not to have as good a home as other Americans. It is lower if he is to be content with driving the same car for ten years, if his son is not to have a college education, if his family is not to enjoy the same quality of food as others, if he is to be without the conveniences that others enjoy, and if the provisions he makes for his family are to be less than those of non-Southerners. If his schools are to be second-rate, and if the public services provided by his state and local governments are to be second-rate, the cost of living is lower. But that well-worn note, "slightly higher in the South and West," applies to many of the things he buys.

In fact, in terms of the share of disposable income required to pay for the basic necessities of life, the cost of living is *higher* in the South. The urban Southerner must pay a larger share of his disposable income for clothing, medical care, and transportation than other Americans. He pays only slightly less for food and housing, despite the substantial gap between income in the South and income elsewhere.

Here again the apologist comes forward. "The South," he says, "is *agricultural*. The per capita income figure does not take into account the food that people grow for themselves and all the other incidents of farm living that the Northerner must purchase for cash."

This is but another myth. The South is no longer agricultural and rural. The urban population of the South is greater than 50 per cent of the whole population. And the part of personal income in the South that comes from farming is less than 6 per cent.

Why should the Southern workman receive less than the wages of his counterpart in the North? Is he not as skillful, as resourceful, as productive? Are not his needs as real, and his hopes as substantial, as those of others? Has he not the same responsibilities to his family and his community? Should he not receive equal pay for equal work? We as Southerners seem somehow to have accepted this condition of inferiority without much quarrel.

Indeed, we contribute to it. In the headlong rush for new industry, we often cheat ourselves. Throughout the South there are "development authorities," engaged in building plant facilities for outside industries with money raised at the taxpayers' expense. Tax concessions are pushed forward, depriving the local community of the benefit of property value enhancement. The new firm is thus subsidized by citizens who can least afford it.

To this tax haven is added the lure of "cheap labor." We seem to be saying, "Come on down, brother. We want to shoulder your tax burden for you. We want you to exploit our people. And when you have done all that, you're welcome to take the profits from our people and our resources back North with you." Is that equality? It is no service to the people of the South to encourage their exploitation as "cheap labor." New industry is beneficial— if it pays a decent wage, and pays its share of the tax burden. Otherwise, new industry can be merely new exploitation, adding a new dimension of inequality for the

South and the Southerner. Southern inequality has persisted too long, and we can afford it no longer.

❊　　❊　　❊

If the South is to stop losing and start winning, our first
goal must be to close the "Southern gap"—to eliminate all
disparities in education, income, public services, health
standards, and economic opportunity. First among the
most effective forces we can apply in this endeavor is
government.

In theory, state governments are best equipped to carry
on the vast bulk of governmental activity because they
are, again in *theory*, closest to the people. In practice,
neither of these theories presently applies. I have previously recounted the sins of County Unit government in
Georgia, and the toils of a grossly malapportioned legislature. While Georgia was unique among Southern states
in the Unit System, the lack of representative government
is duplicated in many other states, and in most Southern
states. A survey of the relative representation of the nation's 3,073 counties showed that Fulton County, Georgia,
whose county seat is Atlanta, ranked 3,073rd before reapportionment. The individual citizen of Fulton County
had less voice in his state government than any citizen of
any other county in the United States. When 15 per cent
of the people of a state are voiceless, as was the case for
Atlantans before reapportionment, it is not surprising that
state government was deaf to their needs.

Until a few years ago, the surest way to defeat a measure
in the General Assembly of Georgia was to have it sponsored by a Fulton County legislator. As a result, our interests had to be "bootlegged" through some small-county

representative, who could, of course, exact his political toll in the process. In former years, before court-ordered reapportionment, a prime criterion for Georgia legislation was: "Does it he'p the farmer?" And many a bill, needed and meritorious, failed because it didn't "he'p the farmer."

Recall that throughout the South, less than 6 per cent of personal income is derived from agriculture. Yet that small sector exercised near monopoly control over the people of Georgia.

All Southern states have burgeoning departments of agriculture. Many have state-subsidized farmer's markets. They have farm-to-market roads. They have special tax rates for agricultural lands. They have special tax exemptions for agricultural pursuits.

But they have no departments of urban affairs. They have no slum-clearance programs. They have no housing programs. Southern states have little protective legislation for the industrial worker. They have little activity looking to the future of the growing regional cities of the South. There are few state programs assisting in the construction of municipal water and waste facilities, or other sorely needed utilities. In education, too, the system works against the city child. In Georgia, for instance, there are two types of school systems, county and independent. The latter are creatures of cities, and within Fulton County is a Fulton County school system and a City of Atlanta school system. Under state law, free school-bus service is provided to pupils of county systems, and denied to pupils of independent systems. Why? Because independent systems exist primarily in cities of some magnitude.

Rural domination is not limited to Georgia, or indeed to the South. Yet its impact upon the South is the more drastic because of Southern inequality. Its effect is to compound that inequality into a doubly unhappy situation for urban Southerners.

Southerners are the foremost victims of malapportionment. But strangely enough, they seem also to be its foremost advocates. When the Supreme Court ruled that both houses of state legislatures must be fairly apportioned, Southerners were the loudest in their denunciations. Southern legislatures were the first to memorialize the Congress, and everybody else, about the unfairness of having to be fair. In the 88th Congress a Virginia Member of the House introduced a bill to deprive Federal courts of jurisdiction in apportionment cases. The Virginia chairman of the Rules Committee pulled it away from the Judiciary Committee, and pushed it onto the floor. It passed by a vote of 218 to 175, with practically every Southerner voting for it. In the 89th Congress, almost every Southern Senator voted for another effort to reverse the Court decision.

It is well to examine carefully the contentions of those who are trying to reverse the legislative reapportionment decision. Advocates of a proposed Constitutional amendment which would permit states to base apportionment of one house of a bicameral legislature on "factors other than population" present an appeal which at first glance seems attractive: "If the people of a state, by referendum, decide that they want to base one house on geography, or historical relationships, or economic factors, they should be allowed to do it. After all, it would be the will of the people because it would have to be done by majority vote in a referendum."

But any referendum would pose a simple "Yes" or "No" to a plan drawn up by presently malapportioned legislatures. As political power is rarely relinquished voluntarily by those in power, it is almost certain that any plan submitted to referendum by such legislatures would continue existing inequities as far as possible. Then, too, the "referendum" might be in the form of an entirely new state constitution, and would embody many considerations other than representation alone. The voter might be hesitant to reject the entire constitution because of dissatisfaction over one portion.

Perhaps such a new plan is only *slightly* unfair. In a few years, population shifts would place every plan out of balance, and the mild disparities of the present would grow into intolerable inequities in the future. Voluntary adjustments would be as impossible then as they were before the Supreme Court ruling a few years ago. The "referendum" proposal sounds reasonable, but in reality it would mean business-as-usual for unrepresentative government.

Advocates of the proposed amendment counter that rural areas are usually sparsely populated and, without some leveling factor, may be in thrall to population centers. They point out that fishing interests of the seacoasts, for example, need balancing with industrial interests in the big cities. They relate the difficulties of covering a wide area of small density, as compared with a small area of high density.

Such arguments overlook the traditional American Constitutional principle that "Governments are instituted among men, securing their just powers from the consent

161

of the governed." If the consent of the governed is diluted or dissipated by political impediments, how then will just powers be derived by the government? And who among us is wise enough to determine the proper degree of discrimination against urban voters, or against mountain voters, or against agrarian voters? Who is to decide which economic interests are to be helped, and which hurt? Who will determine which historical factors will make up the formula for discriminating against which group of citizens?

The antagonists of this controversy were identified by Jefferson many years ago:

"Men by their constitutions are naturally divided into two parties: One, those who fear and distrust the people, and wish to draw all powers from them into the hands of the higher classes. Two, those who identify with the people, have confidence in them, cherish and consider them as the most honest and safe, although not the most wise depositary of public interest. In every country these two parties exist. Call them therefore Liberals and Serviles ... Whigs and Tories, Aristocrats and Democrats, or whatever name you please. They are the same parties still."

There is but one fair rule: One man should have one vote—nothing more, and nothing less. For geography serves only to locate people, history only to guide people, and economic interest only to serve people. Government must represent people. There is no other valid factor.

The states have lost their power and influence in national affairs because they have failed to meet the people's needs. If they are ever to regain their lost prominence, it can come only through effective service, and that can come only through fair representation. The believer in States' rights as something other than a subterfuge for states' wrongs should realize this, and hasten the advent of representative state government.

The same principle—that the way to make representative government work is to make it representative—applies equally to the Congress.

On February 17, 1964, the nation, and most particularly the House of Representatives, was startled by the Supreme Court's decision in the case of *Wesberry* v. *Sanders*, holding that Congressional Districts must be equal in population as nearly as practicable. The holding stemmed from the situation existing in the Fifth District of Georgia, my District, which at that time was the second largest District in the country. The first to react were Southern Congressmen who, in large part, served underpopulated Districts.

Soon, every state will be redistricted in accordance with that decree. Georgia made the change with a minimum of effort. As a result, the people of the old three-county District now have two Congressmen instead of one. Their voice and influence in the councils of the nation have been doubled. They now stand on a par with people who reside in other Georgia Districts. They have achieved political equality in the House of Representatives. Happily, there is no move afoot to subvert this holding. New constituencies will have the opportunity, every two years, to select new representation in Congress. The interests of urban people, long discounted by rotten-borough Districts, will be on a par with the interests of rural people. In this dramatic change in the character and make-up of the House of Representatives, Southerners have an unusual opportunity for Southern progress, and strengthened powers for eliminating Southern inequality.

In the new representation accorded urban Southerners is new power to apply the vast resources of the Federal Government to Southern problems.

The facts are quite plain. The South, economically the poorest region of the nation, needs financial help more than any other region. It stands to profit most from Federal programs. Southerners, accordingly, should support programs which can provide badly needed assistance at home. Yet it is the Southern Congressmen, along with Republicans, who never cease to find reasons for opposing Federal legislation. It is they who decry the Federal tax burden the loudest, who protest Federal "meddling" the longest, and who point out sinister and foreboding implications in the simplest Federal measure.

Yet the facts of Federal taxation and Federal spending contradict them. In one recent year, total Federal receipts were 94.3 billion dollars. Of this amount, 15.9 billion dollars was derived from the South. The national per capita payment to the Federal Treasury was $516. The Southern per capita payment was $311—40 per cent less than the national average.

What happens to the money? On a national basis, the Federal share of all expenditures for government assistance to individuals amounts to 48 per cent, with states paying the remaining 52 per cent. In the South, the states provide 27.7 per cent and the Federal Government provides 72.3 per cent.

In Federal expenditures, the state of Georgia receives from the Federal Government $1.63 for every dollar it sends to Washington. All Southern states receive in return substantially more than they pay.

There are undeniable conclusions to be drawn from

this most favorable balance of payments. On the most selfish level, Federal programs are obviously profitable for the South. The rest of the nation makes a substantial contribution to Southern people with every dollar of Federal money that is sent to Washington.

Those who are interested in seeing the South prosper through the assistance that is available from the Federal Government should welcome Federal programs.

This is a realistic view. Yet, the Southern approach has been largely the opposite: "Why let the Federal Government come down here and take your money in taxes? They send it up to Washington where the bureaucrats waste it, after taking their handling fee off the top. Let's keep our money right here in Kinchafoonee County, where we can see that it's spent right." How long have Southerners heard that rhetoric!

The fact is that a dollar from Kinchafoonee comes back with sixty-three cents interest—after deducting the "handling fee."

There was a time, thirty years ago, when the Southern outlook was different. The nation was then in the depths of the Depression, and the South, being poorest, was hardest hit of all. It was then that a new group of Southerners went to Congress. There was no question then about Federal control, Federal tyranny, Federal usurpation, or Federal blundering. They supported President Roosevelt and the New Deal. They voted for REA, TVA, public housing, the Agricultural Adjustment Act, school lunches, the National Recovery Act, and a host of other measures designed to do what had to be done. That support stemmed from simple economics—the same economics that applies to the South of the 1960's. Southern need is unchanged, comparatively. Yet Southern support of programs to fill Southern needs is pitifully small.

The Federal Government offers a major opportunity for closing the Southern gap. Realistic Southerners will acknowledge this. And their own realizations must be reflected in the representation they send to Congress. If the South is to win, it must see that all levels of government perform at maximum efficiency. Our problems are massive, and our remedies must be applied wherever needed. One effective level of government—whether state, Federal, or local—is not enough. All must labor to eliminate Southern inequality.

Most Southern states need all the help they can find in a host of fields—housing, slum clearance, rapid transit, highway construction, water pollution control, mental health and retardation, hospital construction, medical facilities, school construction, juvenile delinquency, soil conservation, river development, depressed-area aid, water quality control, technical services, elementary and secondary education, and the whole range of new programs available through the Economic Opportunity Act.

Yet how long have state agencies decried Federal intervention, all the while doing nothing on their own to meet apparent need. The rising degree of pollution of the nation's waterways, for example, has received much attention in recent years. Everyone agrees that something must be done, yet very few are doing anything. Finally, in response to pressing need, new Federal programs were mounted. Then came the old refrain of "Federal intervention," and the old cry—"We don't want Federal control!" But the *people* don't want polluted streams! If the Federal Government is willing to take charge where others failed, then it should move without further delay. The important consideration is to see the job done—by whichever instrument of government is capable and effective.

Several months ago I posed this question to a group of Atlanta college students: "If states fail to control pollution, should new Federal measures be enacted?" After brief discussion a vote was taken, with a surprising and encouraging result of 27 "Ayes" and 9 "Noes." Public servants must be directed more to governmental results and less to governmental theory. If Federal money is required to meet a need, then Federal money must be spent. If Federal power is required to eliminate an evil, then Federal power must be exercised. If state money is required to mount new state efforts, or to participate in helpful Federal programs, state revenues must be raised. And local government must not be unduly hindered from joint endeavor with the Federal Government.

The important consideration is that government, at whatever level, act, and that it act in the interest of the people it is bound to serve.

To be sure, there is a natural division of public functions between state and Federal Governments, and a Constitution that prescribes a General Government of limited powers. Yet it is as true today as when Jefferson wrote a century and a half ago, that "laws and institutions must go hand in hand with the progress of the human mind." Surely it must have been farthest from the minds of the Drafters that their Document ever be interpleaded to resist needful and progressive measures, or to uphold and defend outworn traditionalism.

Government must be a major force in closing the Southern gap. It cannot, of course, be the sole force, for government, any government, can be no more effective than the people and the economy from which it draws its strength. It cannot substitute for a stable economy, for an industrious and capable labor force, for a well-informed and well-intentioned citizenry, or for the hard work required of every family to care for its own.

But humane government can act in those areas of human need which remain beyond the reach of private action. Wise government can invest public moneys in public works, thus providing a public benefit that would otherwise be lost. Forward-looking government can fashion long-range opportunities for its citizens which would be impossible without public resources. And only government can impose judicious restraint to prevent aggregations of wealth or power from stifling the ingenuity and endeavor of those not born to wealth or power.

Thus government is but one force, albeit a major one. The land of the South, with all its natural riches, and the people of the South, with their individualism and resourcefulness, are the other.

*   *   *

If the South is to win, all Southerners must have a share in the gains to be won.

Sooner or later the realistic white Southerner must consider the other Southerner, the one whose skin is black. Somehow, his thinking about "the South" must expand to include the *whole* South, specifically that one-fifth which is Negro.

This is not a simple change. All of us were brought up hearing about a "Southern way of life." We knew, from earliest childhood, of the valiant struggle for "Southern rights." We heard men in Congress speaking for "the South." We have seen and heard until we are weary all the charges made against "the South." Yet all of these, the good along with the bad, refer not to the South as 40 million people, but to *white* Southerners. I well recall the scathing letters charging me with that most unpardonable sin, being a "traitor to the South." What South? The South is a land where black men live, too.

The realistic Southerner will see that the South is white-columned mansions and Negro slums, gracious hospitality and rude xenophobia, lazy days along a winding river and long hours in a lint-filled textile mill. It is bluegrass and wiregrass, blue blood and hot blood, country clubs and Ku Klux Klan.

And the realistic Southerner who seeks equality, and hopes to close the Southern gap, will clearly discern another gap, within the South, between white and Negro Southerners.

There are 818,000 families in nine Southeastern states with incomes of less than $20 per week. These states, with 17 per cent of the nation's population, have one-third of all the families in the country living on less than $1,000 per year. Almost two-thirds of all Negro families in the South have incomes of less than $3,000 per year, and one-half live on less than $2,000 annually. One-fifth of all Negroes in Georgia live on less than $1,000 per year; while 25 per cent of Alabama Negroes, 33 per cent of South Carolina Negroes, and 37 per cent of Mississippi Negroes live below this level.

Consider what this gap means in strict terms of economics—confining the inquiry to dollars and cents only. High wages and low unemployment benefit the whole community. High wages mean high tax receipts and expanded public services. High wages mean increased consumer spending, and increased profits for business. Increased profits mean expanding job opportunities, and better working conditions. Low unemployment means low welfare expenditures, and decreased cost of public health, police, and other public services.

Hence full employment, at high wages, is the goal of every modern economy. Unemployment in the South is currently at the reasonably satisfactory level of 4.4 per cent for whites. Unemployment among Negroes is 8.7 per cent. Per capita income for white Southerners is $2,470 annually, compared with $927 for Negroes. Negro income is only 40 per cent that of whites.

This gap has a dramatic impact upon the Southern economy, and is largely responsible for the existence of the Southern gap itself. For instance, if the 360,000 employed Negroes in Georgia were earning wages equivalent to those of whites, Georgians' earned income would increase by 540 million dollars annually. Because consumer demand always runs ahead of disposable income, practically the entire half billion dollars would be spent. According to a generally accepted economic theory that one dollar is spent four times over before going out of circulation, the annual gross product of Georgia would be enhanced by 2 billion dollars. Consumer demands provide 17 million nonagricultural jobs in the South. Increasing Negro purchasing power could easily develop another 2 million jobs in our section. This of course does not include the benefits that would flow from increased self-sufficiency and reduction of welfare cases. The Federal Government now spends 500 million dollars annually in welfare payments in the South. A substantial reduction in these expenditures would come from heightened earnings among those on the bottom of the economic heap.

Even so cursory an examination of the Southern economic structure leads to the inevitable conclusion: the South is poor because the Negro is poor. The South can never attain equality as long as one-fifth of her people live in poverty. The entire economy of the South will continue to suffer because of Negro unemployment, Negro poverty, and Negro dependency. And these factors multiply themselves in their other manifestations: illegitimacy, disease, malnutrition, alcoholism, broken homes, delinquency, crime, slums, drug addiction and the whole range of human misery.

The realistic Southerner needs no humanitarian impulse nor any democratic idealism in order to recognize poverty among Negroes as the chief cause of the Southern gap.

Like it or not, the South's lot rises or falls with the lot of the Negro. The economic alternatives are quite plain. The majority of Southerners, who are white, can continue in the old ways, excluding the Negro from advancement and economic opportunity. Southern resistance can, as it did one hundred years ago, defeat the aims of all the civil rights laws, present and future. The place of the Southern Negro can remain unchanged. To adopt that course will mean that the Southern gap will continue, and perhaps widen, to the continued detriment of all Southerners, and to the continued misery and unrest of Negroes.

That is one possibility. There is another. The Southern gap is in fact the South's great opportunity, for no other section of the country has so vast a reservoir of undeveloped human resources. The Southern majority can resolve to extend real opportunity to the Southern minority. We can help the Negro prepare for full participation in Southern life and the Southern economy. We can help him reach maximum efficiency as a producer and contributor.

To close the Southern gap will require the elimination of those practices and attitudes which have produced and preserved the wide disparities between whites and Negroes. All Southerners, of whatever race, must be encouraged and aided in reaching their full potential as contributors to Southern communities. Particularly, those Southerners on the lowest rungs of the ladder, whether black or white, must be raised to the highest level compatible with their own ability and industry.

Here is our choice. In my view, the moral implication is plain. Notwithstanding, it is a choice that can be made independently of religion, ethics, or morality. It is a choice demanded by economic fact.

❖   ❖   ❖

If the South is to win, Southern politics must be structured upon that goal.

V. O. Key, in his book, *Southern Politics,* maintained that the prime factor in Southern politics was the race issue. Key described the South of twenty years ago, and I cannot dispute his conclusions concerning the politics of that time. Since then, however, two major developments have come about in the South.

The first is the return of Negro suffrage. The second is the re-emergence of the Republican Party. For many decades the Republican Party in the South depended almost wholly upon Negro votes. It was a caretaker structure whose function was to parcel out jobs at the post office when a Republican occupied the White House. Because of the white Democratic primary, Negroes consistently voted Republican in general elections. Under a one-party system, this limited the effectiveness of their franchise to Presidential elections. It was only natural that Negroes should attach themselves to the party which claimed the heritage of Abraham Lincoln, and welcomed them into its councils. Thus for many years Southern Negroes were Republicans.

Even after Franklin Roosevelt and Harry Truman, many Negroes remained committed to the Republican camp. By 1960, the economic record of the Democratic Party was making strong inroads into Republican Negro strength. Still, old ties are strong, and notwithstanding Senator Kennedy's famous telephone call to Mrs. Martin Luther King, Atlanta Negroes voted 60 per cent for Richard Nixon.

Again, in the 1962 Congressional race, Republicans in the Atlanta area relied heavily upon their traditional strength within the Negro community. Negro Republicans were much in evidence, recounting past glories of the party at every opportunity.

By 1964, however, a dramatic reversal had taken place. It will be recalled that the "moderate" wing of the Republican Party took over from the "conservative" forces at the Republican National Convention of 1952. The same change took place in Georgia, and the moderates held control for twelve years thereafter. But in 1964, the pendulum swung back. In a manner reminiscent of the old struggle between the Lily-whites and the Black and Tans of post-Reconstruction days, the latter-day Lily-whites consumed the Black and Tans. At county conventions throughout the South, hundreds of previously undeclared "Republicans" trooped in and routed the old moderate leadership. Nowhere was this more evident than in Georgia. The new state chairman announced that Republicans would do better without Negro support than with it. Goldwater fever was of epidemic proportion. The right wing was now in full control of the party, and the Lilywhites had returned.

The appeal of the Republican Party in the South in 1964 was race—pure and simple. True, many honest Republicans of long standing, although somewhat leery of their Party's nominees, felt obligated to support the ticket. Then, too, there were the economic conservatives who found themselves in full accord with the retrenchment demanded by the Republican platform.

But no one is naïve enough to think that Georgia went from 64 per cent Democratic in 1960 to 54 per cent Republican in 1964 because of economic factors. The old Southern Republicans had depended on the Negro vote. Their successors also depended upon it, but only to frighten whites into voting Republican. The Republican position in the South in 1964 was a new and sophisticated form of racism. The old Democrats of Populist days had mounted the stump to shout "nigger!" The new Republicans disguised the old appeal in new slogans and shibboleths, like "lost freedoms," "Federal dictatorship," and "crime in the streets." Their racism was diluted slightly with an added factor of respectability and the facile subterfuge of conservatism. In Georgia, the Grand Dragon of the Ku Klux Klan pledged his efforts to defeat the Democratic Party, and was joined by his Imperial Wizard over in Alabama. The John Birch Society entered the fray. Thousands of white Southerners, who had profited immensely from Democratic programs, turned to the new white Republican Party. Republicans carried all five Deep South states, picking up one Congressional seat in Georgia, five in Alabama, and one in Mississippi. Had they run more candidates—any candidates—they would surely have won more Congressional seats.

The future of the Republican Party in the South is quite plain. It is destined to supplant the old demagogues on the race issue. It will promise to retrench government efforts at all levels, on the basis of "States' rights and individual freedom." The question for those Southerners who want the South to win is whether Southern Republicanism can serve that cause. Unless there is a radical revision of thought within that party, it will continue to stand for unrepresentative state government and the reversal of the Supreme Court's mandate of one man, one vote. It will continue to oppose Federal programs that can help the South close the Southern gap. It will continue, in the spirit of 1964, to advocate the dismantling of Federal assistance in the broad range of problems confronting an urban nation and a newly urbanized South. And at home, Southern Republicanism will assume the same position on race which Southern Democrats are gradually abandoning. The Democratic white primary was abolished by law. A white Republican Party has come into being through choice and design.

The Southerner can choose between old disparity and new equality for the South. If Southerners demand that the South continue to lose, they will choose Southern

Republicanism as their instrument. The Southerner who wants the South to win will be anxious to see race disappear as the central issue in Southern politics.

Republicanism will have a major impact upon the course of the Democratic Party in the South. What is to become of the Dixiecrat conservative? If he admits to being a Democrat, he is irrevocably branded by Republicans as an intimate of Bobby Baker, an integrationist, a tool of Walter Reuther, a rubber stamp, a Socialist, a do-gooder, a wild spender, and in varying degrees soft on communism. No matter that he call himself a "Southern Democrat," or a "conservative Democrat," or an "independent Democrat." The single term "Democrat" is enough to provoke the full range of Republican epithets. And the Southern Democrat can hardly be more "conservative" than his Republican rival. Even if he competes on "conservatism," what will it merit him? Very little. The Ku Klux Klan has gone for good over to the other side. The right wing, racist or otherwise, are firmly Republican. There is little that any Democrat can gain in emulating the new Southern Republicans.

There is much to lose. Southern moderates are not necessarily advocates of civil rights legislation, or of sweeping changes in social patterns. They are simply Southerners who do not make race-baiting a way of political life. With the rise in Negro voting throughout the South, the Southern Democrat who reverts to the old days of Bilbo, Tillman, and Vardaman will find that he gains no Republican votes, and loses whatever support his party may have earned for him among Negroes. The result is a net loss. Further, Democratic voters who are oriented to the national party program will find it difficult to develop enthusiasm for one who consistently opposes his party's national goals. The field is severely strictured for the old-line Dixiecrat.

Ultimately, the only way the Southern Democrat can move is toward the party's national program, supporting some of it, but still retaining far more independence than Democrats from other sections, where two-party politics is fully developed.

Two-party politics will have a profound effect upon the South's Congressional representatives. The old-line Southern Democrat will sooner or later be supplanted by a Republican of even more conservative hue. The middle-of-the-road Southern Democrat will find himself more and more on the side of the majority of his party on national issues. Southern Democrats in the Congress will move closer to their Northern colleagues, and Southern Republicans will move farther away from the majority of their party. The day may come when the three major divisions in the Congress are Democrats, Republicans, and Southern Republicans.

Just as Southern Republicans have pre-empted the old Democratic standard of States' rights, so has the Democratic Party acquired from them the mantle of Abraham Lincoln.

It was not difficult. I know a long-time Negro Republican who was chairman of his party's committee in a small county adjoining Atlanta. In 1962, the young sophisticates (about four in number) decided to take over the party. Their bitter complaint was that having "old Charlie" as head of the party made it difficult to move. The following year he was eliminated in favor of a Lily-white executive slate. "Old Charlie," for years the Republican leader of that county, is now a Democrat.

Then, too, independent of strict party matters, the martyrdom of John F. Kennedy and the masterly politics of Lyndon Johnson have generated new and strong loyalties among Negroes, particularly in the South. It is a safe assumption that the overwhelming majority of Southern Negroes who will become voters for the first time will be, and stay, Democrats.

This, more than the never-quite-clear Republican objections, accounted for the vigorous Republican opposition to the Voting Rights Act of 1965.

The immediate effect of mass Negro registration in the South is difficult to forecast with certainty. The Negro vote will probably follow the same pattern as that of other minority groups, and initially be cast on ethnic grounds. Thus, at first, almost any Negro candidate will probably receive support from Negro voters. However, as time passes, Negro voters will exercise or fail to exercise the same discretion as white voters. They will make their choice on the same wise or foolish basis as all other Americans. Then, too, as Negro suffrage becomes a reality, there will be less reason for Negroes to cast a "protective" vote. The great and beneficent effect of increased Negro registration will be to eliminate race as a central factor in Southern politics. The day will come in most districts when the Negro vote will be substantial enough to deter racist politics, and to insure defeat of racists by moderate candidates.

That day has already arrived in many Southern cities.

It came years ago to my Congressional District, which is about 25 per cent Negro in registration. It will come to the more remote counties of the South within the next few years.

The demand for racists is already fast diminishing. Those Southern politicians who refuse to believe in equality of opportunity will learn to nurture their beliefs in silence.

This political imperative was illuminated by one of my Southern colleagues during the House debate on the Voting Rights Act of 1965. Listening to the harangues in the well of the House, he remarked somewhat cryptically that it "wasn't too wise for those boys to talk too much against the voting bill." "Which boys?" he was asked. "Those boys that talk with Southern accents," he answered.

Most assuredly, the addition of large numbers of Negro voters will have a profound effect on Southern politics. It is the ballot, in the last analysis, that will bring about the changes so fervently sought by Southern Negroes. True, the passage of the civil rights legislation of recent years has served to eliminate the obvious and legalized forms of discrimination. The events that preceded their passage served to fix the national conscience to a goal of equal opportunity. But respectable Negro registration and active Negro participation in the political process are essential to assure public programs and public attitudes that, over the span of years, will eliminate root causes of inequality.

* * *

If the South is to win, it must deal effectively with those who are determined that the South should lose. Principal among those elements is the Ku Klux Klan, constituting today a major organized force in opposition to Southern progress.

One by one, other less radical and less extreme devices and doctrines, designed to countermand or withhold implementation of the Supreme Court decision of 1954, have fallen. The massive resistance laws of the 1950's are now expunged from Southern statute books. The Citizens Councils, who proclaimed that irate and determined white opinion, along with economic pressures, could stave off compliance, have melted away. Southern politicians who based their campaigns on the doctrine of "No, not one" have revised their speeches. Even Southern Republicans, elected in 1964 on a pledge to repeal the Civil Rights Act of that year, have made no effort to carry out their campaign promises, except in speeches directed to the folks back home. But case followed case, and judgment followed judgment. It is now clear that political utterance and economic practice cannot reverse the pace of emerging citizenship for Negroes.

The Klan, however, offers another alternative—terror. And with the decline of other forces, the Klan has grown in numbers and activities.

Klansmen are oath-bound to keep secret the identity of their fellows. They consider themselves beyond the law. They plot violence wherever it serves their purposes. They carry out deliberate and premeditated acts of terror. Their pronouncements are without restraint as to truth or reality. A few years ago, the Klan was generally considered an object of pity and ridicule. No longer, however, can Southerners afford to dismiss the "Invisible Empire" as ludicrous or trivial. The record of violence and terror of the last few years is adequate evidence of the Klan's motive and potential.

Throughout the South, men are meeting in secret, often unknown to each other except by number. In one Klavern, the Exalted Cyclops declares that there is "work to be done." He writes the names of offenders on green slips of paper and places them in a hat. The hat is passed among the Klansmen, and each picks a slip. Each man drawing a name now labors under a duty to "take care of" that person—by bombing, burning, or whatever means he chooses. He is entitled to select from the membership of the Klavern others who then are duty-bound to follow his orders. This is not the arcane ritual of another fraternal lodge. These men are terrorists pure and simple. Their purpose is terror. Their work is terror. Their strength is terror.

The Klan will remain a grave danger to the South, and to Southerners, until its power is curtailed. The strength of the Klan lies in its secrecy. The remedy will be found in depriving the Klan of that secrecy.

Silent men, dressed in robes and hidden by masks, might make an impressive sight as they march silently through the streets of a small Southern town, following a fiery cross. The Cyclops, Klailiffs, Kludds, and Kligrapps—so long as their identity remains undisclosed—impart an awesome power. But when that same small community knows who is behind the hood, and knows, as small towns always know, "all about" the Kleagle, and the Klokard, and the Klexter, the power vanishes. When it is plain that the men marching through the town have driven there from forty miles away at the request of the local Klavern consisting of three members, that is another matter. And when the public knows the truth about the money problems within the Klan, and the endless disputes over Klektokens and imperial taxes and robe sales, the influence of the Klan will dwindle and disappear.

The question facing each Klan-ridden community is whether elected officials and community leaders will govern its affairs, or whether those leaders will abdicate their duties to unknown pretenders in white robes and masks. It is a hard question in a small town, and there are not many who are anxious to stand up to threats, harassment, and occasional physical danger. Yet that question must be answered by Southerners. The record compiled by the House Committee on Un-American Activities should afford a sound basis for that decision.

* * *

If the South is to win, all her people must join together. There is a community of interest among all Southerners, black and white, rich and poor. It will be the task of thoughtful Southerners to emphasize that common interest, and to unite our people in the face of those who would continue to drive them apart.

This is no simple task. There are inevitable personal consequences that can becloud the view of Southern whites.

Shortly before I first came to Congress, an elderly woman stopped me on the street. "My husband and I voted for you," she said, "and we think you will do a good job for us up there." I thanked her for their confidence, and she continued, "We sure hope you can do something to help us. We've been living in the same house for forty years, and it's all we have. Now the Negroes are moving into the neighborhood, and we don't know what to do. We can't sell it for anything like what it's worth, and we just don't know what to do."

This was not a racist speaking. She was just a lady who lived a quiet life in a quiet neighborhood, and who only desired to continue her days in her old home. Now the changes were affecting her home, and her neighborhood. It was not that she blamed Negroes for seeking better housing. She was only concerned about what would happen to her home and to her investment.

Some communities, North as well as South, have responded to similar situations by rock-throwing, threatening phone calls, and civil strife. Under these circumstances, it is understandable that whites and Negroes alike can lose sight of their common interests.

But both have common desires, which are not mutually exclusive. Both seek adequate housing, in decent surroundings, free from the clutter and filth of slums. Both seek neighborhoods of quiet and repose. Both seek homes for raising children or for enjoying retirement years. The basic problem, therefore, is adequate housing, and adequate living room. And the basic responsibility, therefore, falls upon those local agencies, either planning commissions or housing authorities, who must apply the resources of Federal programs to their own cities and towns.

Most assuredly, it is no easy task, and there is no sure formula for success. But while the immediate solution to such difficult situations may evade us, sound planning and careful execution of housing programs by local authorities can radically diminish, and perhaps some day eliminate, the toils of overnight changes in neighborhoods, with their toll of lost investments, heightened tensions, and lasting suspicions.

Given the heat and ferment of racial incidents, such as disturbances over "block-busting," little men with little minds can sometimes touch a responsive chord among their hearers. The Grand Dragon of a Southern state recently declared: "The niggers have the N.A.A.C.P. The Jews have got the B'nai B'rith. The Catholics have the Knights of Columbus. What has the white man got if it ain't the Klan?"

The question, propounded in ill faith by one who would reject any response, nonetheless deserves an answer in good faith.

It would be well to understand something of the concern with which Southern whites regard the advancement of Southern Negroes. Indeed, the white Southerner on the lower economic level sometimes considers himself a forgotten man—forgotten by the Supreme Court, by the Congress, by the President, by the rest of the nation, by the local economic interests, by the clergy, and, sometimes, by his own representatives in government.

It is his school which is most heavily integrated. It is his neighborhood that is most easily subject to "block-busting." It is the public pools, where his children swim, that are mixed. It is his job that is threatened by the equal employment laws. And the public accommodations which he can afford are, for the most part, the only ones Negroes can afford.

"What's the white man got if it ain't the Klan?"

The white Southerner has the South—rich in natural and human resources, and ripe for full development. He

184

has the prospect of Southern equality, and the elimination of the old disparities that have placed him, as his fathers before him, at a disadvantage with respect to the rest of Americans. He has the opportunity to be an important part of the economic and industrial expansion of his region, to his immediate personal benefit and the lasting benefit of his children. He has the prospect of better schools, better housing, better health services, better jobs, and better transportation.

For the aspirations of Southern Negroes are not vastly different from his own. They, too, share his hopes and ambitions for their own children. They, too, need decent wages, decent homes, and good schools. They, too, need the training and education that will equip them to make their own way in a complex and competitive society.

Indeed, all white Southerners—manager and worker, rich and poor—have everything to gain by the diffusion of education, the increase in general prosperity, the reduction of unemployment, and the rise in living standards among Southern Negroes.

The advancement of the Negro will make possible the further advancement of the whole region. From his increased wages will come increased profits to Southern business. From increased profits will come more and better job opportunities for all. From reduction in Negro unemployment will come reduced public assistance costs. From the Negro's increased stability and independence will come lower public expenditures for all kinds of public services. And from a developing awareness of a common cause for Negroes and white Southerners will come new importance and new influence in the political and economic affairs of the South and of the nation.

What's the white man got? Eight million Southern Negroes, who are moving upward. If we join in a new community of interest, the lot of all Southerners will be immeasurably bettered. If we are kept apart by the old divisions and distrust, the Southern gap will continue, to the abiding detriment of all Southerners.

*   *   *

Swift change is upon us. The current is moving. That tide, taken at its crest, leads on to fortune. If it passes us by, we will spend the remainder of our days in shallows and miseries.

The duty now rests squarely upon Southern leaders—for only they can lead.

The old ways have been dissolved in outward form. The legal barriers which have kept our people apart are now lowered. The South, black and white, faces a momentous decision. Will we move together, or find new devices for staying apart? Will the Ku Klux Klan and the Black Muslims succeed in nurturing within the new generation of Southerners the old hatreds? Will Southerners seek the Old South—or turn to building a New South?

That decision cannot be made in legislative chambers, or by chambers of commerce, or by central labor organizations. It will be made by the people of the South—by Boy Scout troops, Rotary Clubs, boards of stewards, fraternal lodges, Masonic Orders, trade associations, union locals, literary societies, presbytery meetings, county political committees, planning commissioners, county boards, credit unions, bridge clubs, service societies, military reserve units, garden clubs, music guilds, alumni societies,

Junior Leagues, Little Leagues, and the host of advisory committees that relate to practically every function of government, from courthouse to White House.

The decision will be made day by day, and deed by deed. It comes with the quiet handshake extended to the Negro Christian who presents himself at the door of the white church on Sunday morning. It comes when the Negro maid moves her bundles onto her lap so that a white girl may take a seat beside her on the bus. It comes when a Negro stops his car to help a white motorist stalled along the roadside. It comes when the white workingman passes the salt down the lunch counter to his fellow laborer who is black. It comes in the ready acceptance by white children of the transfer student whose skin is dark. It comes when the girls in the office treat the new colored secretary like any other new secretary. It comes when an able Negro is elected secretary of a local union.

It comes when Southerners accept other Southerners only for what they are—good or bad, wise or foolish, able or inept, venal or honest—regardless of color.

✿　　✿　　✿

The South can lose again, just as we have lost for the past century. If we ignore Southern history, we will relive it. If we remain divided, we will suffer anew the old consequences. If Jim Crow is our goal, and equal justice our enemy, the South will lose.

Will the South win? I believe it will. The people of the South are young, and new generations grow more realistic. There is a grace and honesty about Southern people, and a basic good humor that attends most of their personal relationships. There is a deep pride in the South, and a genuine desire for Southern progress. There is a love of country, a respect for history, and a basic optimism.

These personal traits, so widespread among Southerners, will serve us well when we fix upon new and worthier goals.

       ❖   ❖   ❖

The preceding has not sought to proclaim moral imperative, but rather to demonstrate practical opportunity. Its province has been history, not ideals; politics, not ethics; economics, not morals. Yet, there is a matter more compelling than history, more persuasive than politics, and more rewarding than economics. There is the matter of simple justice.

Our fundamental charter declares all men created equal. Our basic religion declares us our brother's keeper. But the demand for justice rests not alone on legal precept or theological tenet. It is a demand that spans creed and clan, age and continent. It speaks now as it has to prophet, saint, and patriot—and to unnumbered millions of men and women throughout all time.

It wells up from the heart as plain truth and clear duty. Let right be done.

DATE DUE

OCT 12 '67		
DEC 6 '72		
GAYLORD		PRINTED IN U.S.A.